WHY WOMEN AND MEN DON'T GET ALONG

WHY WOMEN AND MEN DON'T GET ALONG

A GUIDEBOOK FOR WOMEN *FRUSTRATED* BY MEN'S BEHAVIOR

HOW TO GET WHAT YOU WANT AND IMPROVE YOUR RELATIONSHIP WITH THE OPPOSITE SEX

CAROL L. RHODES, PH.D.

NORMAN S. GOLDNER, PH.D.

Published by Somerset Publishing Co.

Published by Somerset Publishing
P.O.Box 4386
Troy, MI 48099

Printed in the United States of America

Library of Congress Catalog Number: 92-81365

Library of Congress Cataloging-in-Publication Data
Rhodes, Carol L.
        Why women and men don't get along:
        A guidebook for women frustrated by men's behavior
        Carol L. Rhodes, Norman S. Goldner
        p. cm.
        Includes Bibliography
1. Women-Attitudes. 2. Women-Psychology. 3. Social interaction.
I. Title. II. Title: Why women and men do not get along.
III. Title: A guidebook for women frustrated by men's behavior.
HQ1206.R6 1993   302.1   QB192-572

ISBN: 0-9632309-6-4

CONTENTS

Chapter 6 Biology and Personality as Factors in Gender Problems

Dedicated, With Love, To Our Families And To Our Children

Seth	Rob
Sasha	Colleen
Aaron	Bill

ACKNOWLEDGEMENTS

There are many people to thank for their help with this work:

Our clients have provided the core of our insights and understandings. We have great respect for people who are able to acknowledge that they have a problem reaching their goals and then choose to educate and change themselves rather than follow an unproductive path.

Family, friends, colleagues and students made vital contributions to our work with both their encouragement and ideas. Caroline Calvert, Colleen Rhodes, Sandra Palmer, Ron Koenig, Julie Breidenstein, Seth Goldner, Frank Rodriguez and Sheridan Robson all read and commented on one or more chapters.

Dr. Bernard Green, as Director of the University of Detroit Clinical Psychology program, was so enthusiastic about the ground we were breaking that he invited us to teach a graduate seminar, *Women and Men*, which allowed us to share our ideas with PhD students from whom we learned much in return.

Most of all, we acknowledge one another. We have taught and worked together as marital and family therapists for many years. We developed many of our insights about gender differences and how to apply them positively from our own marriage. This book is still another delightful collaboration that enriches our lives.

FOREWORD

About The Authors

Your authors are: wife and husband; devoted companions; lovers; friends; co-therapists; individual, marital, divorce and family therapists; co-authors; and co-sojourners through life. Those who know us well understand that we have an exceptional relationship which includes our children, our families and friends.

Part of our success is due to "chemistry," part to the utilization of understandings we've developed in our relationship and as marital therapists. "Chemistry" is a foundation of our loveship and of our ability to work harmoniously together. Chemistry is that difficult to define but powerful set of forces that seems to bring people together. It's like charisma in both its power and its vagueness. When two people naturally mesh, it makes living easier.

Chemistry is a desirable factor in a marriage but not it's not sufficient to assure a good and lasting relationship. There are many other variables that affect relationships.

One variable we've found to be subtle but extremely powerful is *gender identity:* An individual's subjective experience and self-conception as being either girl or boy, woman or man. Along with biology and the culture's definition of how women and men should behave, gender is a potent determinant of male-female relationships.

There are other very significant factors at work in our relationship. Professional training and experience have added to our understanding of human behavior and ability to get along in our marriage. In addition, our clients have been rich sources of understanding that we have learned to apply to our life as a couple.

For example, we have learned to fully respect one another. "Respect" (Webster's Dictionary) includes honor and esteem, high regard, deference, consideration, avoidance of intrusion, and courteous regard. Respect is enhanced through an understanding that each person is unique, and that each woman and man is strongly determined by her or his genetics and their culturally assigned roles.

If you aren't ready to accept the *individual humanity* of the person with whom you want to share your life, how can you possibly create a good relationship? Instead, you'll always be in a struggle with the other person because they'll surely defend their right to self-esteem.

To have a successful relationship, we recommend you select a person you respect. If you do not respect members of the opposite sex, then when you enter into a relationship, you will have much to overcome.

Others, including members of the opposite sex, are as OK as you are. You were not "placed on this earth" to make the other person over into who and what you think they *should* be.

That presumption of one's own "rightness" is what we call "gender conceit." A fulfilling relationship with the other sex requires that you honor the sexual and gender differences between you including their individual uniqueness.

Gender Sensitive No-Fault Therapy

This book began as a monograph for our clients, as a companion piece to the therapeutic approach we have developed over the years and now call **Gender Sensitive No-Fault Therapy.**

Gender Sensitive

Therapy is "gender sensitive" when it takes into consideration two of the most important determinants of a person's life:

1. The biology of their sex;

2. The social, cultural and psychological components of each person that defines their identity and their role in life.

We help couples focus on the "natural" separators between them. They learn that women and men are different and that the **gender gap** between them is to be **bridged**, not eliminated. Bridging is difficult but rewarding; the elimination of differences is impossible and frustrating.

No-Fault

The "no-fault" property of the therapy is based on our observation that virtually every couple entering counseling is battling about which of the parties is to *blame, guilty*, at *fault*, or *wrong*. Nothing consumes them more than assigning fault and blame to one another while trying to preserve their own self-esteem.

We guarantee you that no good flows from making one person a winner and the other a loser! If this happens, both parties are losers. There are no optimum marriages based on competition for and struggle over who's right and who's to blame. Every negative transaction leads to individual and relationship harm.

Our basic philosophy is to view the role between people as problematic and to search for mutually agreeable solutions.

When a couple understands they have distinct qualities as women and men, they don't have to assign blame. It is a relief to our clients when we focus on their natural differences and help them to see how certain problems proceed from the way they deal with these differences. Energy can then be used to harmonize the relationship.

Idealistic or Practical?

Much of what you read in the following pages has been "tested" in our relationship and has served us well. We have applied it to our work with couples with positive results.

For example, we know that men generally dominate public conversations when both sexes are present. Especially in the early stages of a relationship, men control communication. Women allow men to set the conversational topic and defer to them, drawing out men's stories. Here's an example of how this situation can be modified once the couple understands gender dynamics:

If he interrupts her before she's completed her thought, instead of taking this as a personal affront and firing back a caustic remark or withdrawing and pouting because she feels diminished as a person, she can say:

"Sweetheart, we know that men are more assertive than women. But, I didn't get to finish what I was saying."

"Woops! honey, I did it again. It's hard for me to drop that habit. Please, finish what you were saying. I'm interested."

Here's another example:

She might want to know how he is "feeling" about something or just what his emotional state is in general. He does an inventory of his inner-mind and finds: *Nothing* seems to be going on. He has no awareness of any feelings. His lack of awareness of feeling doesn't square with her perception of his mood but, she learns not to feel "left out." She knows that he, as a male, has more difficulty identifying and communicating his feeling states.

She also knows, from experience, that this man—trained in gender styles—will talk when he becomes aware of what his emotions or feelings are. Sometimes, after she's asked, "Is something going on?" and he says, "no," he'll come back minutes or hours later and tell her that he is indeed aware—thanks to her querie—that something was bothering him. He'll share it with her and consider himself fortunate to have a companion who can help him to experience his emotional life.

Idealistic? Perhaps, but in fact we've helped many couples arrive at understandings of the role of gender and sex in their lives. Behavioral, cognitive and emotional changes have taken place which benefited the client because they reached their own goals.

Why Women And Men Don't Get Along will start you on a path to clear understandings of yourself and how to get what you want out of relationships—while the other person gets what they want, too.

This volume contains many statements about women and men that are global and categorical. We have done this to avoid endless qualifications. Our intention is to characterize gender differences and interactions that are normative, not absolute in their occurrence. The material in this book applies only to those women and men who fit its generalizations.

Our portrayals of people's lives in *Why Women and Men Don't Get Along* come, for the most part, from our day-to-day clinical work with patients as they struggled to improve their lives and from observing the lives of those around us. The names and descriptions of individuals and couples have been significantly altered to preserve their privacy.

INTRODUCTION

Men and women are different. What needs to be made equal is the value placed on these differences.
—*Virginia Woolf*

Is Gender Important?

Here's a simple test to demonstrate the power of gender in people's lives, **including your own**:

1. Have you ever met someone and **not** noticed whether they were female or male?

2. Having noticed which sex s/he belonged to, did you find it did **not** matter to you in any way?

3. Can you claim to **understand** members of the opposite sex as well as you understand your own?

If you answered "yes" to these questions, you are rare. Nearly everyone answers "no" because whether you are a man or a woman matters in almost every situation. Gender is virtually never ignored. Everyone is assigned a position in one "sex" or another and it lasts for life. It is not optional.

Sex assignment and its importance vary from one culture to another but it is always of great consequence for each individual.

Gender: Now You See It Now You Don't

Sex and gender are forces in our lives that are obvious, yet little understood. Note how we talk to one another about the opposite sex: "You know how men are"; "Boys will be boys"; "That's a woman for you"; and so on. We seldom appreciate the influence of gender differences in our relationships despite our claims to the contrary. Because we cite the differences between us doesn't mean we realize **why** and **how** we are different, or how these differences impact upon our lives, or what to do about these differences when they trouble us, or that we **respect** the differences between us.

This book will clarify sex and gender differences and show you both how to **accept those that can't be changed** and to **shape those that can**. Throughout this book we will repeat, in various ways, the following powerful and illuminating themes:

1. There are **biological** differences between the sexes such as size, weight and physical strength that are subject to modification but only within strict limits. Genetically determined biological characteristics are generally fixed and unalterable.

Some **Culturally** determined differences between the sexes can be altered through learning and social action. However, when culture leaves its imprint, it often takes on the same unchangeable character that biology has.

After an earthquake destroyed buildings in Cairo, Egypt in late 1992, a man was "miraculously" found alive after three days in the hot rubble. His wife and children died because they refused to drink their own urine. In short, a cultural dictate was followed though it cost them their very lives!

If you know which differences—biological or cultural—can be changed and which are relatively permanent, you are in a better position to both understand how women and men differ and what, if anything, can be done about it.

With knowledge and correct action you can change negatives into positives and get what you want and deserve. Our major goal is to help you enhance your relationships, and to do so in ways that are least frustrating and most effective.

2. One of the most important ideas you can use in the pursuit of your interests is the *interaction factor* which holds that:

Insignificant differences between women and men are magnified and become huge gaps in understanding when women and men engage in social relationships or are in each other's presence.

The interaction factor will explain why men and women seem to be so alike and yet have so many difficulties getting along together. Whatever differences there are between the sexes, and no matter how slight they are, when women and men interact the differences are amplified.

The *interaction factor* will explain why, in specific situations, slight differences between women and men are magnified into chasms and why the way back to understanding and cooperation between the sexes seems like an impossible maze.

If the *interaction factor* is so powerful, why don't couples realize how different and sometimes incompatible they are from the beginning of their relationship?

A. Boys and girls are born into a world where their status and roles are predetermined. Natural individual differences are minimized by cultural prescriptions which squeeze each sex into different identities and roles.

B. Girls and boys are gender-role separated at such an early age that by adolescence or early adulthood they are estranged and have few clues as to how to behave with one another.

C. The first stage of female/male coupling is characterized by **"idealization"**: Each sex wants to see the other as an answer to their dreams, needs, and desires. Any characteristic which doesn't fit the idealization is minimized or denied.

You undoubtedly know people who were "blinded by love." After some weeks, months, or years into the relationship, they're shocked and disappointed when they learned the "truth" about the other person. Ignorant of specific gender differences, partners focus on the personality shortcomings of their partner whereas the sex/gender phantom is actually the culprit.

Since sex and gender are so embroiled in our identities and so thoroughly built into our social, political and economic lives, it's difficult for us to separate the effects of our sexual identities from other issues and problems.

3. From the moment we begin our learning we develop powerful **world views** which create mental road maps that become our arbitrary **reality**. Reality is socially and psychologically constructed within the limits of our genetic code—though you may have difficulty accepting this idea. Once these habits of perception and action are established early in life they are highly resistant to change. (How many of your New Year's resolutions do you keep?)

Although women and men live in the same physical world, each has a world view specific to their gender. Each gender's world view is different enough to cause problems between them. Women and men have a strong tendency to think, feel and behave *as if* their ways and those of their own gender are "right" and inherently superior.

Even when our views and their rigidity is pointed out to us, even when it is causing us great harm, we hold stubbornly to our ways. Some of these patterned behaviors are referred to as "addictions," things that are bad for us that we'd like to alter but which resist our will to change them.

Women and men have their own ways of communicating, acquired in childhood and reinforced throughout their development. These communication differences are magnified when the sexes interact and significantly interfere in relationships both at work and at home.

Communication Problems: Cause or Effect?

"We can't communicate!" is the most frequent complaint couples make in marriage counseling. On closer inspection, what they mean is, "If my husband (wife) would communicate *the way I do*, our relationship would be fine."

From early childhood, women are more verbal than men. Does this make them better communicators than men? Not unless talkativeness is equated with "good communication." Women and men communicate better with members of their own sex. Most of the complaints about communication are directed across the sexual barrier.

If either sex had a basic problem with communication it would appear everywhere in their lives, not just with members of the opposite sex. Women and men are equally skilled at communication but in different arenas. Women are better at talking about their feelings and relationships; men are more inclined to speak about sports, politics, and the outer rather than their inner world.

These differences are so little appreciated they take on the status of "secrets." Here are some "secrets" about sex and communication; ideas which will help you reduce your frustrations and make you more powerful in the world:

Secret One: Men and women communicate well with same-sex members but seem to speak a different language with the opposite sex.

Women are known as better communicators (in relationships) but males are often skilled communicators in their occupational roles. Men have great discussions with one another about politics and sports, and their jobs often depend on their communication ability. Something "mysterious" and negative happens when women and men try to make themselves understood to one another.

Secret Two: Although women are noted for their willingness to discuss and reveal their feelings, men's range of feelings seem to be limited to anger, humor and lust. This is because they are trained to deny most of their emotional life.

Is it true, as many people believe, that women have more **insight** because they deal with a fuller range of emotions? In fact, both women and men are necessarily subjective and have no monopoly on personal insight. They both make the assumption that their way is the right way.

Insight is defined as an awareness of why one feels, thinks, and behaves in particular ways. *Talking*, without insight, is ineffective communication in the arena of relationships.

Secret Three: Women and men are different in the ways they think, feel and behave. Each gender has learned to approach issues and the opposite sex in such significantly different ways, they confound one another. Women are more interested in how people get along and will sacrifice some of their interests to accomplish social objectives.

Men think "logically," especially in terms of objective problem solving. They learn that women look our for their welfare but they don't know how to keep women and others constantly on their own minds. (Brain physiologists are now suggesting that brain structure makes it likelier that men keep fewer things in the forefront of their minds than do women.)

Men prefer to deal with issues that have clear boundaries and are therefore solvable. They often avoid emotional issues and *sticky* human relations that are not so easily or directly understandable and manageable. ("Look, there's nothing we can do about it so forget it!")

Women place a priority on social matters whereas men are more disposed toward the "mechanical world." Women live more in an "inner world", men more in an "outer world."

The Frustration Factor

We all have complaints about others and would like them to change. But, how practical is this goal? It is hard enough to change yourself let alone others. If you assign blame and responsibility to others for your unhappiness, you give them ultimate control over your life. If you can't be comfortable or happy or secure unless others do as you want them to, they need only refuse and you lose.

You will get more benefit from your efforts if you change yourself rather than others. A frequently raised objection to this suggestion is the fear that the one who changes is the loser. If the other person doesn't change and we do, aren't we the loser? Haven't we sold out and given in? The authors argue strongly against this view! Instead, the more responsible you are for what happens in your life, the more successful you will be.

Prioritizing For Change

Both in our clinical practices and in the literature, we find that women have more complaints about men than men do about women. Whether you have many or few complaints, to achieve the results you desire it is necessary to establish, clarify, prioritize, and communicate your needs, wishes, wants and goals.

You must: know your own values; assess the likelihood of achieving desired changes; test your assumptions by trying them out; and use your energy and talents to get what you want. To illustrate, you may have a naturally high sex drive while your partner's is naturally on the low side. Is it a reasonable goal to bring the other person up to your sexual level? Is it even possible? We doubt it. Give it your best shot and see what happens. Then, adjust your expectations and your behavior accordingly.

A more realistic and rewarding goal may be to bring your respective sexual interests as closely into harmony as possible. If it's not possible to reach a satisfactory, mutual state, you will have to prioritize: Just how important is sex in the marriage? Some sexually dissatisfied partners value the family aspect of the relationship so highly that they decide to maintain the marriage without adequate sex.

Some women submit to sex to maintain their base of economic security. There are many reasons for adapting to less than ideal circumstances. There are just as many reasons for changing your circumstances if you cannot get what you need and want.

Three Power Ideas To Live By

As you read on, keep the following interconnected ideas in mind:

—Knowledge of your self and others will provide alternatives that will free you from

your interpersonal pain. Gender is one of the most important determinants of human behavior.

—There are differences between you and the opposite sex. Learn to *bridge* these gaps; do not try to eliminate them.

—Seek change in yourself, not in others. Changing one's self enhances personal power whereas trying to change others gives them power over you.

In the chapters that follow we'll focus on gender and sex differences which lead to relationship difficulties. In each chapter we will show you how these gender based problems interfere with your life and we'll show you how to overcome them.

Chapter One, MALE AND FEMALE DIFFERENCES, focuses on how sex related characteristics affect relationships in ways both positive and negative. Once you understand the powerful role of gender in your life you gain control of your own fate and are better able to solve relationship problems. You will have choices you don't have now. You will be more effective in your life than you've ever been before.

1

MALE AND FEMALE DIFFERENCES

People say, "Vive la difference" but [the difference] is more like a cruel joke created by God. Men and women desperately want to be with each other, but at the same time they can't stand each other.

—*Rob Reiner*

Joan And Brad: Different Perspectives

The relative calm of Joan and Brad's twenty-three year marriage was shattered when Joan discovered Brad's affair. Shocked by the discovery, Joan's ensuing rage and emotional turmoil brought to the surface buried resentment, disappointment, and unfulfilled needs. Now neither of them could overlook the problems which had been brewing for many years.

Married twenty-three years, Joan, 45, and Brad, 44, sought marriage counseling because of Brad's extramarital affair. Naturally, Joan and Brad had very different experiences of the affair. Joan focused on the betrayal and Brad sought to put the whole mess behind them. That wouldn't do. The affair had to be dealt with.

Joan's Side

It was spring when Joan called for an appointment. She explained that she had been upset for over a year and couldn't pull herself out of an alternating state of anxiety and depression. In desperation, Joan decided to seek help from a therapist.

During her first counseling session she spoke in a rapid, tense, but composed manner, her hands tightly clasped together. "Last year at this time I was happy and I felt good. My family was doing well, and my husband and I were getting along. I liked my job as a med tech [medical technologist] and had fun with my friends at work. There weren't any big problems. In fact, I felt as if I had it all.

"Then," she said, "I discovered life at The Waffle Shop." A woman called Joan's home to find out if Brad was O.K. He hadn't been to The Waffle Shop for several days and this worried the caller. "He generally comes in every day."

Joan had never heard her husband mention a "waffle shop." The telephone voice also asked, "Are you Brad's sister?" Joan was stunned. At that moment of realization, Joan's placid life exploded: Brad was in the midst of an affair!

Joan continued, agonizing over every word: "I still can't believe this happened, that he did this to me! I'm totally baffled because Brad didn't appear to be unhappy in the marriage. I've been a loving wife, always going along with what he wanted. Our sex life was good—or so I thought. Now I realize I didn't know then what he really wanted and I still don't know.

"I fear he'll hurt me again. I watch him like a hawk for clues, for signs that he's doing it again. I'm miserable with him now, jealous of his every move. But, at the same time, I try to calm myself thinking, 'I don't care.'

"I don't know who he is. I've lived with him for 23 years and he's a stranger. He says he's sorry but I can't believe him. It's as though the affair is over in his mind so any thought about it should be erased from mine. But, I *can't* get it out of my head. It goes around and around: why, when, how, where? I know it's stupid to keep thinking about it. It's been over for a year but it simply won't leave me. I don't want a divorce or separation. I want peace of mind.

"We tried marriage counseling when it first happened. He quit after three sessions because he couldn't stand my anger. The only thing that has kept me sane has been talking to my close friends. Now I need more than that. I need to resolve this problem and I don't know how."

From the moment Joan discovered Brad's infidelity she felt "mentally tortured." In a searing instant of psychic pain, Joan's orderly, inner life became a roller coaster of jealousy, anxiety and fear. Brad, in contrast, was relatively calm.

Brad's Side

Brad agreed to give marriage counseling another try because Joan insisted. He seemed baffled by his wife's "over dramatization" of a "situation that just happened." He presented the affair as a quirk, as having no meaning to him. It was an "unfortunate accident." He acknowledged his infidelity had been a blow to Joan, but in his mind the affair wasn't serious: "The woman doesn't mean anything to me. Joan should be over it by now. How long is this going to continue? How long will I have to pay for it? I've done everything I can to show her I'm sorry I hurt her."

Brad viewed both the affair and his wife's reaction to it with annoyance and detachment, as though it was a problem to be solved and dealt with "logically." Having admitted his violation of the marital vows he now wanted the problem to go away. "I am not interested in any other woman. I love Joan. She's been an ideal mother, a wonderful wife. The sex I had with the other woman was just that: Sex. It wasn't what I would even call an affair."

Crises Are Opportunities For Change

Crises provide a powerful motivation for change and growth but few people welcome a crisis into their lives. The hackneyed phrase "no pain, no gain" is true; a crisis, with all its turmoil, is an indicator that something is wrong and change is needed. However, when it's *our* critical event, it's difficult to see how good things can come from it.

Because of their marital turmoil Brad and Joan had an opportunity to reevaluate their relationship and approach their problems in a fresh way. They could now *decide* how to improve their life together, not just get along as best they could while finding their satisfactions elsewhere.

Before the crisis, Joan could not recall when Brad had been emotional. He even disliked emotional displays in others. She learned to hide her feelings in response to his disapproval. The safety in accepting Brad's logical approach allowed Joan to avoid her own confused feelings. Using his voice as her own, she would second-guess herself, put herself down. She was often afraid to tell him what she thought because he would out-talk her and point out the "errors" in her thinking and judgment.

When Joan learned about Brad's affair, she felt *she* was a failure. Just as being an obedient daughter had not brought her a pat on the head or magically solved her parents' problems being a good wife hadn't protected her marriage. Using this convoluted reasoning, she felt responsible for the affair and the sorry state of her marriage.

During the year of marital therapy Joan and Brad's life settled down and they resumed some of their social routine. Still, Joan's mind was mired in the affair: "Where did I go wrong? Did he love me? Why did he do it? Is he still doing it? Will he do it again?" She wanted to ask Brad these questions but she was afraid to keep bringing up her doubts and fears because he became so angry. Brad said things like, "Don't be ridiculous! You shouldn't feel that way. You misunderstood. Forget it, it's not important." He would quickly end any conversation that even hinted at the affair or contained any emotion.

One way we manage to accommodate ourselves to the unacceptable is to ignore it as best we can. Joan decided long ago that Brad was unaffectionate, did not understand her, and gave no thought to what she needed. Joan said, "I accepted the situation and put it in the back of my mind."

However, when Joan found Brad had love enough to give to someone else her hurt intensified. Feeling vulnerable and low in self-esteem, her needs to be loved, held, and soothed became a desperate, overwhelming desire. She felt empty, trapped, and alone.

Joan had known for years there was something wrong in her life but she learned to ignore "it." The problem was not concrete; she could not, for example, point to physical abuse or alcoholism. Instead, Joan experienced a vague sense of uneasiness and dissatisfaction within the relationship. Her husband worked and was responsible; they had a good home and family. So, why should she complain? If she did, who would listen and make things better for her? Brad and Joan lived together yet they were *a gender world apart.*

Gender Gap: The Grand Canyon in Marriage

The differences between women and men are *magnified* in their relationships. Precisely because sex and gender affect us so subtly they are powerful forces in our lives. Joan and Brad brought these subtle but crucial gender differences into their marriage. Differences were played out in who took responsibility for the relationship, the emotional caretaking, intimacy, sex, money, and power.

Relationship Responsibility

Joan tried to be everything to everybody in the family. She worked full-time and took responsibility for the children because, she reasoned, her husband's sales job required long, erratic hours so he could not be expected to help much in the house. Joan fixed meals, cleaned house, drove the kids to their doctors, school activities and classes. She took the major responsibility for running the family unit. In short, she performed her female role. When the affair surfaced, she was already programmed to assume that if she had been a better wife, there would not have been an affair.

Women are taught to take responsibility for the relationship. If the relationship fails, they blame themselves. For example, the wife commonly asks questions about the other woman: Is she pretty? What's her figure like? How old is she? The wife then measures herself against the "other woman" to explain why her husband sought what he needed outside of the marriage. She believes if she'd been younger, prettier, less involved in the household, or more exciting, he would not have strayed.

Money

When Brad wanted an expensive sports car Joan protested, then she gave in. After all, he brought in more money than she did so how could she deny him the fruits of his labor. He always got what he wanted—with or without her consent or opinion. Joan admitted that even when she disagreed with his decisions, she felt he should get what he wanted because, even though she brought money into the household, he was the "breadwinner."

Money is a pivotal form of power. Our culture is arranged against women because the importance of homemaking is devalued; it does not produce anything that can be sold or used as collateral. Money talks—loudly.

Power

Clearly, Brad was the power in the household; everyone danced around him. Joan always asked him before she made a decision but he rarely consulted her. He seemed to do whatever he wanted. When he became angry, he intimidated others with his temper. His displays of barely controlled rage, loud verbal attacks, and clenched fists usually carried the day. These rages imply that: physical violence might follow the display; it is legitimate for one person to behave in a threatening, irrational manner; and *out-of-control anger will get you what you want.*

The person who controls the thoughts, feelings, and behaviors of others has power. Without sufficient *personal power*, including psychological independence from Brad, Joan was unable to stand up to him.

Emotional Care Taking

Joan took care of the emotional environment for Brad and the children by doing anything she could to keep life on an even keel. She kept her feelings to herself so that Brad would not be upset. She was the sponge absorbing her family's hurts and disappointments. She received little in return.

She'd made efforts to be understood and cared for, too, but neither the children nor Brad were prepared to respond. She coped by blaming herself for expecting too much and accepted her role. She buried her own needs and disappointments but like a toxic dump, dissatisfaction seeped into her life.

Intimacy

Joan wanted touching, hugging and kissing. Brad, who was seldom touched as a little boy, had not learned to touch others in a loving way. He avoided displays of affection just as he avoided signs of weakness. Joan learned that to expect physical displays of love or to ask for affection was an invitation for intolerable rejection. She learned to do without intimacy.

Sexuality

Surprisingly, both Joan and Brad agreed that their sex life was "excellent." They believed they had sex more often than their friends. Therefore, their "excellent sex" had more to do with quantity than with quality or real satisfaction. As the therapy progressed they were able to face the truth.

Sex was Brad's sole expression of intimacy. This caused Joan to feel used. Since Joan had learned not to complain directly about her dissatisfactions so her sexual experience wasn't open to discussion or improvement. This is all too typical in marriages. Sex becomes a tool in the power game. To maintain the stability of one's self-image and a stable interpersonal life, sex isn't talked about.

Moreover, Joan maintained the illusion that men knew everything about sex and should be deferred to. Any sexual problem was attributed to her inadequacies. She perceived Brad as sexually superior to her. Another block to Joan's sexual satisfaction was her feeling that a woman who actively sought sex would be seen as a slut or a whore—one who "knew too much" about sex.

Therapists are not surprised that married couples talk so little about their sexual needs and feelings. Sexual performance and adequacy are tied up with each individual's self-esteem. Consequently, couples are afraid of sexual discussions. A few bad experiences trying to talk about sex can make it a taboo subject.

A Happy Ending For Joan and Brad

Eventually, Joan and Brad broke through the barrier of Joan *versus* Brad and established Joan *with* Brad, Brad *with* Joan. Until the crisis of the affair, they took each other for granted and devoted little attention to improving their relationship. They'd been unaware of how gender contributed to their problems; they blamed themselves or each other.

Once they recognized their differing needs for intimacy they worked together to find mutually satisfactory solutions and their relationship improved significantly. Joan accepted lovemaking as one way Brad expressed intimacy. Brad, in turn, realized Joan's reluctance to initiate lovemaking or ask for affection had been ingrained in her socialization as female. Now he understood that she yearned for closeness and affection even though she was passive about it.

Joan began to speak to Brad about her needs instead of building up anger and hurt when he didn't magically foresee what she wanted. Once Brad clearly understood Joan needed attention and consideration he began a "love campaign" with words and deeds (cards and flowers) to both reassure Joan and demonstrate his underlying feelings. Brad was rewarded with Joan's focus on him and the marriage.

Part of their marriage counseling sessions had been devoted to working through feelings about the affair. They learned an extremely important approach to resolving the bitter feelings about the affair: They focused on the **why** of the other woman rather than **what** had happened.

It is understandable that Joan would want to know all of the details of the affair but eventually she understood that this was like taking poison: the specifics of where, when, and how only tattooed the pain in deeper. Brad and Joan learned to deal with **why** their marriage was too weak to bear the honesty of their respective feelings.

At times the pain resurfaced. In counseling Joan learned to talk about these feelings calmly and to realize they would pass. This couple learned methods of managing their emotions so they could express them safely. They came to **respect** one another, to recognize the other person's inherent right to think and feel differently.

One of the most valuable outcomes of therapy for Joan and Brad was their experience that they could face a formidable a problem and work it through. It made subsequent difficulties much more amenable to early notice and resolution.

Too Much Emphasis on Sex and Gender?

Not every difficulty in a relationship is caused by sex and gender differences.

Nevertheless, gender is a subtle, powerful variable in people's lives and problems. Everyone is aware of how different women and men are, yet the effect of gender on relationships is poorly understood. Even when couples realize their problem has something to do with the differences between women and men they still have difficulty putting this vague understanding to use. We need more detailed information.

Sex refers to biology and anatomy. **Gender** is largely socially determined. Women and men are assigned to a gender role and then act out masculine or feminine behavior as prescribed by society and culture (and influenced by biology). Gender constitutes the core of our self-conception and much of our behavior for the rest of our lives.

A person of one sex (genitally, anatomically) who experiences themselves as a member of the "opposite" gender is going to experience terrible internal conflicts. Consider what it would be like if you woke up tomorrow with the mind of a woman but the body of a man!

The social and psychological consequences are awesome when a person realizes that their gender—their conception of themselves as man or woman—is different than their sexual anatomy. Men have mutilated their penises and women have cut through their breasts in disgust at the awful feeling of being a member of the wrong sex.

Gender is established at both the conscious and unconscious levels; we regard ourselves, treat others, and expect to be treated by others consistent with our sexual identification and gender roles. In all known societies people believe and behave as though sexual differences are real and meaningful. Therefore, they *are* real and significant in their effects. In short, **gender matters!**

Inherited Vs. Learned Gender Characteristics

There is considerable controversy about how much of our sexual identity we learn and how much is due to biology. What role does genetics play in determining the differences between men and women? Are females and males basically the same or different? The two major philosophical positions concerning similarities and differences between the sexes are *minimalism* and *differentialism.*

Minimalists

Minimalists argue that except for reproductive specialization, *women and men are equal.* They admit there are some differences in height, weight and strength, but even these are overlapping. Some women are taller, heavier, and stronger than some men. Women swim the English Channel faster and theoretically can run longer distances because of their fat reserves and metabolism.

Minimalists are correct when they maintain that:

1. There are no basic, genetically determined personality or intellectual differences that inevitably translate into behavior.

2. Personality is determined by socialization and culture with some contribution from genetics.

3. There is no justification in nature to excuse the subjugation of one sex by the other.

Differentialists

Differentialists believe there are dramatic differences between the sexes that are both genetic and learned. They cite differences in such things as language skill, spatial perceptions, mechanical aptitude and mathematics.

Undeniably, women and men are physically distinct. Each sex has a specialized function in reproduction; they are different in their average size, weight and strength. Males are not only larger and stronger, they are more aggressive and potentially more dangerous than women.

Both Minimalists and Differentialists agree that if there are personality differences between the sexes, they are mainly due to culturally produced roles and norms. *Women and men learn to be different and thereafter experience each other as different.* There is no scientific foundation for the claim that personality is genetically determined.

Are Women And Men the Same Or Different?

Let us return to the question: "Is too much made of gender differences?" Minimalists would say, "Yes, much too much." They have a strong point here, especially in an industrial society in which there are so many power-assists (self-starting automobiles, electric motors, hydraulics, etc.) that any difference in physical strength is minimized.

If women and men are so similar, why do they experience each other as so different? One answer is: **Women and men act differently in same-sex groups than when they are with members of the opposite sex.** This is referred to as the *interaction factor*. Differences may not be apparent until the sexes are socially mixed. Why is this so?

Eleanor E. Maccoby (1990) and her colleagues made an important contribution to understanding why seemingly slight variations in women and men are so consequential:

> ...Behavioral differentiation of the sexes is minimal when children are observed or tested individually. Sex differences emerge primarily in social situations, and their nature varies with the gender composition of dyads and groups. Children find same-sex play partners more compatible, and they segregate themselves into same-sex groups, in which distinctive interaction styles emerge (p. 513).

In other words, when women and men are measured individually for differences in personality and mental performance—with cultural biases and learned behavior taken into consideration—they seem much alike.

However, when they interact their differences are magnified!

One cannot predict what men and women will do, feel, or think when they are in mixed company simply by knowing who they are as individuals. To use an analogy, neither sodium nor chloride taken separately will taste good but together they make *salt*. Something similar happens when men and women get together; they take on new characteristics when they interact.

To illustrate, we recently had lunch with a professional man who is usually charming in a quiet way. He's a good listener, has a gentle manner, and has a good sense of humor. When the waitress took our order, he made suggestive remarks that discomforted all of us. The waitress was flustered and annoyed but trapped in a situation where her job demanded that she tolerate crudeness. Even in hindsight, we had no way to predict that this otherwise gentle man would be so rude to a woman.

Maccoby's research reveals that gender differences begin at an early age. Here are some of her findings based upon comparisons of the actions of boys and girls in same sex and mixed-sex groups:

1. Young children playing in same-sex pairs were equally social with one another but were less social when playing with a member of the opposite sex. (The average age of these children was 33 months.)

2. Children as young as three were asked to approach other children of the same

and then of the opposite sex. Girls stopped farther from boys than from girls—a sign they exercised caution when nearing boys.

3. Girls at play were not passive in girl-girl pairs but stood aside when paired with boys, letting boys monopolize the toys.

4. A study of young children revealed that at 4.5 years they played three times longer with same-sex partners than with those of the opposite sex. This preference increased to the age of eleven.

5. If children are permitted to segregate themselves by sex they will do so. Deliberate attempts to integrate children in play activities meet with resistance— they prefer same-sex groupings.

6. The strong tendency for children to segregate by sex is independent of the type of play activity.

7. Children can be integrated when adults set up cooperative tasks for them. Girls seem to need the assurance of adult supervision if they are grouped with boys.

Why do even young children prefer members of the same sex? Maccoby cites boys' rough play and competitiveness, behavior that girls prefer to avoid. Also, girls' efforts to influence boys with polite suggestions meet with failure. Boys do not take low keyed suggestions seriously; girls are likelier to do so.

Boys seek to influence others by making demands. Since boys do not act reciprocally with girls, girls prefer to avoid them. Maccoby believes these early patterns are modified but carried into adulthood. A couple we worked with illustrates this pattern:

> Brenda, a 28 year-old computer sales manager, feels that Van, a 32 year-old divorced print shop owner, is pressuring her. Specifically she feels uncomfortable when he demands too much of her time. The pressure frightens and annoys her but she doesn't know how to handle the situation.
>
> When she lets him know she needs time to get her thoughts in order he responds by assuring her he'll do anything she wants. Then he promptly channels the conversation so that she ends up talking about *his* concerns instead of *hers*. ("Enough about me," the joke goes, "how about you, what do you think of me?") The struggle between them revolves around his fear of "losing her" and her fear that she'll be smothered by his neediness.
>
> According to Brenda, she doesn't want to lose him so she doesn't want to totally discourage him. She's also afraid to "hurt his feelings." Van misinterprets her ambivalence as a signal to persist until he gets his way.
>
> Van is aggressive and assertive about what he wants while Brenda finds herself giving in to his strong needs—although she prefers to have time to herself. We suggested to her that she might get better results by telling Van she wants "time out" saying she would phone him when she was ready to. However, she wasn't ready to be so assertive.

Van and Brenda struggled over differences that developed in childhood. He's not influenced by polite suggestion and Brenda isn't comfortable asserting herself in the relationship. She backs down when he becomes aggressive.

Deborah Tannen (1990), a linguist, makes an argument similar to Maccoby's: Boys and girls grow up in different language worlds. Women, she claims, speak a language that revolves around intimacy, cooperation and affiliation whereas men's language and orientation focus on independence, competition and status. Women get angry when men refuse to do household work. Men are likely to resist the suggestions of women since men signify their independence by giving directions instead of taking them.

One of our female friends handles this problem tactfully. She says that if she asks her husband to take the garbage out, he's sure to forget it or give reasons for not doing it. She gets her way when she says, "Sweetheart, if it isn't too much trouble and you're going out to the garage anyway, and if you remember, would you take the garbage with you?" He then complies because he feels he's in control.

The Interaction Effect

A couple's relationship simply cannot be understood by looking at each individual separately. Something important happens when people interact with the opposite sex.

The interaction effect is quite apparent in marital therapy. We find that our clients express themselves and behave differently in individual interviews than when they are together. To make headway in the treatment, we often have to arrange separate interviews to interrupt the couple's destructive posturing toward one another. For instance, if couples are asked in each other's presence, "Do you love him/her?" they often give a different answer than they do in private. This was true of Candice and Carl.

Candice shifted uncomfortably in her chair when I asked, "Since you filed for divorce, how sure are you the marriage is over and nothing can save it?" Candice paused, then leaned even further away from Carl.
"One hundred percent sure," came her reply. "No question whatsoever. I've begged him for years to go to a marriage counselor and his only reaction was to tell *me* to go to therapy because I was the one who needed it. Now that I've filed for divorce he insists that we see a therapist."
Although Candice sounded convincing, there was something in her voice that signaled less certainty than her words. She agreed to my request that we meet privately for one session.
In private, she began by holding to her position that she wanted a divorce. "He's never changed and he won't change. He thinks he's the boss. I'm out of here!"
If he did change, would that make a difference?
"Possibly, but I know he won't. At least I don't think there's much of a chance this leopard will change his spots. I just can't take the chance of thinking he'll change and being disappointed. ...If I thought there was some hope, maybe I'd try."

In our joint session, Candice said she wanted a divorce. With her husband present she couldn't soften her position and therefore chance losing her resolve. Once we were alone we were able to explore her motivations and fears.
Some stories do end happily. Carl's recognition of Candice's concerns nearly came

too late since Candice insisted on a separation. Paradoxically, their separation allowed each of them to break some of their old habits and to develop a new style with one another.

During the separation, their major interaction focused on co-parenting. This took the pressure off their relationship and provided a more neutral but important arena of cooperation.

Each of them dated others but after eighteen months they were getting along so well they decided to "date" each other. Carl is now genuinely attentive; Candice expresses little anger and feels more confident. They decided to give the marriage another chance. Presently their relationship is better than it had ever been before.

Will The Sexes Ever Be Equal?

Equality is such an important part of the American ethos that we look for it everywhere. Will women and men soon be equal? We think not. Dominance and submission contribute to the gap in understanding between the sexes and increase the problems women and men have relating to one another. Once these patterns are institutionally established and learned in each individual's life, they're hard to eradicate.

We believe that male dominance can no longer be justified by survival needs but that it will nevertheless persist. Once incorporated into a cultural system, any pattern tends to persist. What social mechanisms foster this continuation of inequality?

Culture Perpetuates Inequality

Even before a child is conceived, parents are programmed to raise the sexes differently. Girls and boys are dressed in different colors, given different toys, are expected to do different things, are touched and spoken to in gender–specific ways. For example, a boy is handled more energetically while a girl is cuddled and protected. Fathers are rougher with boys, gentler with girls. Mothers talk more with girls than boys and encourage boys to be independent. Boys are expected, even encouraged, to engage in adventurous behavior ("boys will be boys") whereas girls are protected and kept under supervision and closer to home.

More women are now receiving more education and are getting better jobs at higher pay. However, men are still well ahead in the professions and business while women more often enter service occupations such as nursing and teaching.

This sex–specific socialization begins at birth but is especially true from preadolescence on. Boys are supposed to be tough and not cry; girls can be emotional and express themselves. Girls may emulate some male behavior and be "tomboys" (until adolescence) but if boys emulate girls, they are likely to be accused of homosexuality or femininity.

A cardinal rule for boys who want to become men is: **"Don't be like a girl!"** Males who are in any way "feminine" immediately lose status in the male world. They're also not highly valued for marriage by women.

Which Differences, What Consequences?

Here are some differences between the sexes that we will explore in the following chapters.

1. **Emotionally**, men are trained to repress or to avoid a wide range of feelings in themselves and others whereas women are taught to concern themselves with emotional states. In a heterosexual relationship a female has to struggle to have her emotional needs met.

   Males are simply not trained to pick up on emotions or nuances of behavior. Males are raised to overlook feelings, to deny tender and loving emotions in both themselves and others. Women and men even grieve differently. Studies show that women are better at reading the subtle cues people give off. Whatever goes on inside them, males show less emotion.

2. Men think about and act out the **sexual impulses** that are a constant part of their lives. They have sexual thoughts and feelings many more times during a day than women do. Women are likelier to have periods when they prefer not to have sex. Men are allowed to be openly sexual, even encouraged to be sexual by their peers and the culture. They may, for example, stare at women's bodies without self-consciousness.

   Women know how to sneak looks at men without being detected. Women generally need more foreplay and a loving atmosphere to enjoy sex. Men are not so subtle. Males can erect and perform sexually in a matter of seconds. Women are schooled in presenting a sexual appearance in the way they dress and make themselves up but they are simultaneously taught to repress their sexuality. Men tend to touch women sexually, pinching and squeezing breasts and buttocks. Women, feeling invaded, often object to these intrusions. Men then feel rejected and withdraw feeling hurt and angry.

3. Relating **intimately**, nurturing, caring, listening, fostering and allowing emotions—all of this is women's work. Women take responsibility for relationships and the emotional well-being of others. Consequently, males expect nurturing from women long after their childhood.

Men keep their emotional lives hidden—even from themselves. The women in their lives, whether wife, mother, sister or girlfriend, are tuned into men's needs, feelings and thoughts.

Sex, an aspect of intimacy, often keeps women and men from being socially and emotionally close. Women often complain that if they hug or kiss their men, men respond sexually rather than with intimacy. Consequently, women have to think first before touching and often forgo it because touching invites sexuality rather than closeness.

4. Women are usually **dependent** on men for money and power. Men are seemingly independent economically but they are often dependent upon women for understanding, caring, nurturing and "mothering." Men and women are trained to be dependent in different ways. Women are to be taken care of in the material world; men are to have their inner, emotional lives nurtured by women.

5. Men and women have different amounts and types of **power** in relationships. Men have more power in the world and women admire and are attracted to worldly success. Males are taught to take action; women are encouraged to be patient and reactive. Women are more likely to hesitate, think things over, and proceed cautiously or indirectly.

   Men solve problems from a law-and-order perspective. Women solve problems according to who is involved and whether someone will be hurt or benefited.

6. **Money** represents different values to men and women. Men are more likely to rely on money for power and see money and its distribution as a power tool. Women are the family's chief consumers but they often make less money than the male and are dependent upon men for both buying power and approval of what they buy. Women's need for male approval also reduces women's power.

7. Many **personality traits** are associated in the popular mind with either masculinity or femininity, traits such as passivity, aggressiveness, sociability, empathy, and self-esteem. Moral reasoning, interests, perceptions, listening habits and reactions to stress are different for men and women. (We don't believe that one sex's morality or reasoning or any other characteristic is *better* than that of the other gender's; only that there are *differences.*)

8. Women are comparatively **self-conscious**, have questions about their thoughts and acts and have serious reservations about their bodies and appearance. Men are generally more confident in their presentation of themselves and have fewer concerns about their bodies and appearance.

These and other matters of crucial interest to women who are having difficulty in relationships with men will be discussed in succeeding chapters.

Summary

Biology and culture interact to produce the differences that we focus on. Some readers might prefer to believe all sex differences are learned and therefore can be changed by new values and learning. Learning is irrefutably important to human behavior but we do not believe biology can be discounted.

Whatever the basis for sex differences, once the infant is born and sex is assigned, the social role for that sex is taught and enforced by custom and law. One usually behaves the expected way if the role is established early in life and is consistently reinforced. By the time a child is three it has a fixed sexual identity. Some authorities argue this occurs before birth or before the child reaches one year.

In summary, biology and culture are the primary determinants of sex and gender. They both play a role in how our minds work and how we act out the cultural and societal prescriptions for being male and female. Whatever the origin of male and female differences, *people act on the belief that male and female differences are fixed and natural.* Therefore, differences become a social if not a genetic reality.

The next chapter explores the emotional differences between women and men and how emotions contribute to relationship conflicts.

2

EMOTIONS

If you were to probe inside the guy psyche, beneath that macho exterior and the endless droning about things like the 1978 World Series, you would find deep down inside, a passionate, heartfelt interest in the 1978 World Series. Yes. The truth is, guys don't HAVE any sensitive innermost thoughts and feelings.
—Dave Barry, (Humorist)

Liz, one of our clients, agrees with Dave Barry that men do not have any "sensitive innermost thoughts and feelings" but she doesn't find this amusing. It reminds her too much of Ralph, her husband of fifteen years.

"If we have a discussion about our problems it's only because *I* want to talk. He *never* starts a discussion and he almost *always* says, 'I thought everything was O.K.' As we try to talk things over, I get frustrated and more emotional inside. Then it bursts out; I either cry, get mad or both."

Liz, a 36 year-old beautician, is adept at drawing out other women's thoughts and feelings. In fact, she finds her customers eager to share their feeling and lives—in intimate detail—in stark contrast to her husband who *never* knows how he feels and seldom wants to share his thoughts.

Liz was dressed in the latest fashion with make-up, nails and hair done to perfection. However, her mascara began to run and her nose turned red as tears of frustration and anger streamed down her cheeks. Liz was choking back her tears as she said, "He infuriates me. He doesn't show his emotions—if he has any. He just kind of stares at me as though I'm speaking a foreign language. When I press him for how he feels he's either silent or he says, 'I haven't thought about it.' It enrages me! If I fight back he accuses me of being *'overly emotional'* and he withdraws even more.

Liz's story demonstrates one of the principle emotional differences between women and men: Women express a full range of emotions whereas men repress most of theirs. As a woman, you may have felt more than once that the male in your life was oblivious to your feelings, or he did not want to deal with your feelings, so he:

    a. Changed the subject
    b. Left the room
    c. Ignored your feelings
    d. Insisted that you "stop crying," or
    e. Became angry in response to your
       feelings.

Women find men's emotional patterns frustrating because they are so *different* from their own. The distinct emotional styles of women and men mix like oil and water. In reaction to a woman's "emotionality" men may first show some tolerance and compassion while simultaneously feeling superior as they play "caretaker."

Soon, they try to suppress women's emotionality with such advice as: "Forget it," "It doesn't matter," "Don't take it so hard,"

"Crying won't help," "Look at the bright side," and a variety of other techniques intended to avoid the discomfort which is activated in the presence of emotions other than lust, anger, or humor.

A simple way to test these generalizations is to observe couples attending movies and plays that arouse deep feelings. Men try to hide their tears or fears while women openly display theirs. If he notices tears running down her cheeks or any other outward display of emotion, he laughs, shows disdain, kids her, or tries to quiet her down—all the better to control any feelings he may have and to reduce emotional contagion.

There is a symbiosis, a mutuality, in this arrangement in which women express feelings and men deny theirs. *The male benefits from the woman's emotional expressions even as he tries to subdue them.*

Through the female's expression of feelings, the male—without having to openly "feel"—vicariously experiences emotions and simultaneously maintains his manly calm while avoiding the danger of tapping into his emotional reservoir. He lets *her* feel and express emotions for him. Or, he quashes his emotions by teasing her or trying to shame her into stopping her display. He may show his anger or disgust so that his *masculine* feelings become the issue: "Oh, we'd better not do that. You know how angry Harry gets!"

Students of human behavior are convinced that women and men are capable of the same emotional range but that: 1. Cultures dictate which feelings are allowed and under what circumstances and to whom; and 2. There is some evidence that men's brains are less sensitive to emotions. What are the rules for emotional expression for women and men in our culture?

Emotional Differences and their Origin

Distinctive emotional and feeling patterns are established from birth on and are shaped by cultural norms. Males learn to equate the expression of emotions—except anger or humor—with weakness and femininity. Females are raised to express their feelings (other than anger) and attune themselves to the emotions of others. This is especially true of close relationships, as in the family.

Tricia complained that her younger brother was one of the men in her life who took advantage of her. Tricia was getting "sick of it" and wanted to know what to do. He borrowed and wrecked her car. He accumulated traffic fines that he did not pay with the result that Tricia paid for his attorneys and bail him out of jail. He borrowed her property and failed to return it. He made promises about getting his life in order which he never kept.

What about her parents? They lived in another state and had stopped enabling him years ago. Why didn't Tricia stop her co-dependent role? From her perspective, he "needed" her too much to suddenly drop him. She couldn't bring herself to stop though she knew it would be best for both of them.

Tricia was captive of her trained-in capacity to focus on others' feelings as well as her own. As is often the case, there's little reward and severe frustration in this pattern.

Boys are discouraged from developing the part of themselves that is gentle, nurturing and caring. They receive direct prohibitions against emotionality (or any other "female" trait). Being a boy means, above all, **not acting like a girl**.

For example, boys are expected to tolerate pain. If a young boy cries, his mother may comfort him but she also gives him the message—however subtle—that "boys don't cry." Fathers, brothers, teachers, and playmates may allow the boy a brief period to recompose himself if he shows weakness. Then they kid or shame him into hiding his feelings. If that doesn't work, fathers—even mothers—have been known to give the little rascal something to cry about.

Boys learn that males who admit their vulnerabilities suffer consequences, the most serious of which is a challenge to their sexual identity as males and inclusion in the world of men. Some cultures allow men to act like women; they may be excused from the hunt and they can gather wood and do the things that women do. Cross gender behavior is not allowed in our homophobic culture.

One of our friends is a physical therapist. He tells us men come in for rehabilitation of painful injuries and typically declare that they can "stand the pain." He tells them to stop kidding themselves because it's necessary to

admit the seriousness of the injury and to
follow the treatment plan. Male bravado, which
is founded on denial, complicates the recovery
process.

Men are encouraged to deny their pain.
Turn to the sports page in your local paper and
you'll find a story about an athlete who has
"come back" too soon from a serious injury.
Athletes are lauded for "playing over their
pain." Only sissies refuse to play sports because
of something like a fractured leg. "Finger
dislocated? Here! [Pull, twist.] Now get back in
there!"

A male member of our family injured his
knee seriously enough to require surgery and
rehabilitation. He joined the Special Forces
and re-injured it. Mustered out of the service
he became a ski patrolman and injured it again
and had another surgery. He reports this
without undue emotional distress. This is the
way a real man behaves.

Females are also shaped by their culture and
its gender prescriptions. Being nurturing and
emotionally tuned in to others is something
that is expected of females from their earliest
years. They are traditionally socialized to be
kind, to be thoughtful of others, to give in, to
avoid fighting, and to pursue passive activities.

Little girls' toys prepare them for family
activity: baby dolls, doll houses, and pretend
kitchens. As girls mature they are given dolls
with elaborate clothes, beach cabanas, doll
houses, and other trappings of domesticity. A
trip to the toy department reveals that the
women's movement and androgyny have had

little influence on toy specialization; it's still dolls for girls and trucks for boys.

Emotionality usually intensifies during adolescence. Frequent, abrupt mood swings go hand in hand with the teen years. During this period adolescent girls enrich their emotional range whereas boys learn that to be a real man, a "cool dude," emotions have to be kept under control—especially any that are identified with weakness.

Girls learn that emotions—even those that are intense and unbearable—come and go. Feelings and emotions continue as acceptable parts of their lives. Boys learn to be frightened by emotional expressions other than aggression or a few other male-approved emotions. Thus, adolescent girls and boys learn distinct emotional patterns that are carried into adulthood and further separate them.

Tom and Barbara exemplify divergent female/male emotional patterning.

Tom and Barbara, both in their twenties, asked for marriage counseling because they were convinced that communication was their problem. Although both Tom and Barbara's work requires good communication skills—Tom is a salesman and Barbara is a customer service representative—they are unable to talk effectively to one another.

This couple had what Tom called a "crisis" after Barbara mentioned that Tom seemed remote and she wondered if it had anything to do with her. Tom blurted out, "I'm not sure I want to be married any more." Barbara was devastated. She cried, argued, withdrew, cried some more, and eventually campaigned for outside help. She was continually distraught and couldn't think or talk about anything other than her fears that the marriage was in danger. Eventually, Tom agreed to counseling.

During the first session Tom refused any serious discussion of his views. We shared our understanding with him that men find it very uncomfortable, even dangerous, to deal with their feelings—especially when the stakes are high. To his credit, he then asked for an individual session.

When we met alone Tom's rigid posture betrayed his anxiety. After our initial hello's and small talk, Tom fell silent. Eventually, I said, *"What are you feeling?"*

"Nothing. I don't feel anything. I just think I shouldn't be married."

*"If you're not **feeling** anything, perhaps you have **thoughts** that go with this idea about leaving?"*

"I don't know. I think she would be better off without me. So would the kid."

"Because?"

"I don't know."

"What feelings are you having as you talk about ending your marriage?"

"I don't know. I don't think I have any. I don't want to hurt her. This is hurting her."

"Is it hurting you?"

"I don't feel anything. Nothing comes to me. Maybe numbness."

Tom was not consciously aware of his emotions. Several months of therapy revealed that the more anxious Tom became, the more he adopted the appearance of being totally in control and the deeper his depression became. He worked so hard to control his emotions that his body became almost rigid and he barely moved his lips when he talked.

Tom knew he was unhappy in the marriage and wanted to do something about it. He

described himself as "anesthetized." Any
feelings that threatened to get through were
suppressed. In truth, emotions figuratively
boiled inside him.

Individual sessions gave him enough insight
into his male pattern of emotional control so
that he was eventually able to share his feelings
with Barbara. She had very strong reactions
when he shared his views of their marriage.
She would interrupt, cry, and contradict him.

Sessions with Barbara were necessary to
convince her that she could not simultaneously
ask for information and drench Tom in her
anger if she wanted him to share his thoughts
and feelings. Thereafter, the therapy was more
effective. Tom learned that withholding his
feelings and thoughts was counter productive
for both him and the relationship.

Several months after therapy this couple's
gains were still evident. They reported
difficulties but Barbara and Tom were
confident that they could continue working
them out. They cited understanding of "natural
gender differences" as one their most
important accomplishments.

Expressing Emotions

Training, Shaping and Stifling

As necessary and inevitable as emotions are
to human survival and relationships, the
expression of emotions can be a problem.
While our emotional capacity is inborn, society

and culture shape how it will be expressed. In social situations and intimate relationships, there must be a mechanism to moderate emotions and feelings. Without controls, emotions would overwhelm the individual and would make social life difficult, if not impossible.

For example, we watched a football game in which a player seemed to go berserk when he was fouled. He was ejected from the game. The sportscaster commented that this player gets so excited before the game he hyperventilates, i.e., his breathing accelerates out of control. In short, his emotions take over and diminish his effectiveness. Occasionally a hockey player becomes enraged, loses control, and uses his stick as a weapon, seriously injuring another player.

Emotional control training typically begins in the family. It is necessary for individual family members to keep some of their feelings to themselves and to moderate others. Some families develop a style that allows the males to be expressive, to say what they want to anyone else in any tone of voice they choose while the females must keep themselves in check.

In other families, the females are the emoters and the males are relatively silent. When one or the other family member has a license to emotionally kill and others have to keep their own counsel, there is likely to be "powder-kegging," a storing up of anger that will eventually burst through.

There are productive ways to express feelings. If we recognize our own personal style of emotional expression and are respectful of

our mate's emotional style, we can make
positive choices regarding our emotions and
when, where, and how to express them. If we
don't control our feelings and their expression
it complicates social life. Paradoxically, women
are permitted a wider range of feelings but it's
not always acceptable to air them.
Leona Helmsley comes to mind. In late
1989 the media mockingly anointed her the
"Hotel Queen." She allegedly ruled the hotel
with an iron, and perfidious hand. When she
was being tried for income tax evasion, it also
appeared that she was prosecuted for her
"haughty" and "nasty" disposition. Women are
taught not to act or speak in an *aggressive*
manner, especially in public. Women are
permitted to be more emotionally expressive
than men, but anger and aggression are to be
avoided. An aggressive, emotional display,
acceptable in business*men*, may not be
tolerated in businesswomen. A double
standard? Yes.

Men are allowed to be bossy, even nasty, to
get the job done. On the other hand, they are
strongly discouraged from showing any
emotions that display vulnerability or
weakness. Men are allowed to give a good "ass-
kicking" but they are not allowed to cry in
public. They learn to hide their weakness-
revealing emotions from themselves and
others.

Men: Letting Their Hair Down

Would we all benefit if men let their
(emotional) hair down? If a man cries in the

presence of a woman, a woman might think, "Wow, he allowed me to see beneath that hard shell." Or, she might declare him to be a "wimp" or unmasculine. Women are not always clear or consistent about what emotional patterns they desire in men.

Exhibiting tender feelings is expected of women and prohibited for men. If a man does reveal himself by sharing his feelings, he may believe he has compromised his masculinity and lost his power and authority. The other person—especially a woman—may suffer from the backlash as he tries to restore his position as "the strong one." A male who cries will feel weak—as a woman might—and he knows that society seriously frowns on a weak male. That's why he's learned to hide his feelings and block them from his awareness.

In the political world, a candidate or official who cries is perceived as showing a weakness and his or her suitability for office is seriously compromised. Senator Muskie (D. Maine) made that mistake when he cried because his wife's reputation had been impugned by a rival politician. Senator Dole may have caused himself subtle political damage when he sobbed and choked back the tears in his farewell to President Bush. That ended his efforts to win the presidential nomination.

A woman may apologize for her tears but she also understands that her status as a female is consistent with emotionality so she may cry in public without loss of status—unless she aspires to a position in the male world. This is not true for men. If a male authority openly cries, the judgment against him is severer.

Although it seems to most women that we all would benefit if men were emotionally free, in a society that requires males to be stoic, cool, calm, and collected, think of how difficult it is for men—for anyone—to check or hold back emotions most of their lives, then to display them at other times. If emotional expression is to be expected of men, shouldn't we equally require that women suppress their emotions? In fact, isn't it better to allow each gender (and person) to be true to their own ways and to **respect** them as they are?

Changing Emotional Patterns

When it comes to expressing your feelings and emotions, it can be a "damned-if-you-do or damned-if-you-don't" choice. If you express your anger when you feel it, you may get rid of some of your frustration but damage those around you. If you have lots of feelings and show them to others, they may avoid you.

Another hazard in expressing feelings such as anger is that they feed upon themselves. If you give in to your depression, it deepens. People become *more* angry as they ventilate their anger, not less. True, some people who have violent outbursts of anger or temper tantrums thereafter feel relief. However, those who have been the target of the anger may remember it for hours, days, or a lifetime.

Various emotions are used to control others. Karl kept Jane in her place with his anger:

> Karl, forty-seven, trained his wife of twenty-three years to watch out for his anger. To maintain relationship harmony, Jane, forty-five, carefully thought out any of her own desires or suggestions before speaking to Karl and arousing his wrath. Her own frustration would build up over time until she had an "out-of-control cry-a-thon."
>
> Jane had been a dutiful stay-at-home wife and responsible mother. However, when her youngest daughter was a high school junior she decided to do something different with her life. She mentioned to Karl that she would like to take some college courses.
>
> His angry and unempathic response was, "I worked hard to keep you satisfied over the years. Now that we can spend some quality time together without the kids you want to go to school? I didn't know I was such an ogre and a failure as a husband. Where have I gone wrong?"
>
> Jane sought therapy for help with her dilemma. After six months in therapy Jane's thinking cleared up. She recognized discussions with Karl were always dominated by his thoughts and feelings, a tactic that had confused her in the past. When Karl got angry her mind went numb and she instinctively switched from whatever her concern was to keeping him calm.
>
> Jane eventually mustered the courage, and the resolve, to tell Karl exactly how he had not satisfied her needs. Predictably, he raised the emotional ante. Jane, fortified with insight into his emotional blackmail, refused to back down during his tirades. Karl then substituted sullenness for anger. Nevertheless, Jane enrolled in college without his blessing and was relieved to find Karl eventually accepted her decision. He realized he cared for her and that he had to modify his attitudes

and behavior to preserve the relationship. Her change short-circuited the old pattern. It wasn't back to business as usual just because Karl had decided that he'd tolerate Jane's return to school. Having suffered Karl's emotional tirades for many years there was no turning back for Jane. She completed a degree program, found employment, and on that day served Karl with a divorce complaint. Unfortunately, too much damage to the marriage had accumulated over the years. Karl was left puzzled and embittered—he'd seen the light but it was for naught. He, like many others, wake up too late to save the relationship.

To Express Or Not to Express?

To Express

It seems reasonable to opt for the expression of feelings. Otherwise, they are bottled up and will come out in destructive forms. How feelings are shared is critical. It should be done with "I" statements: "This is how *I* feel...," "When *I* face this kind of situation, here's how *I* experience it...."

"*You* make me mad," and other such accusatory statements create defensiveness. Your message will be lost. But, shouldn't you be able to express yourself as you please? Of course you can if you insist but there are consequences for everything. (Ask yourself what your priorities and goals are. That should dictate your behavior.)

Both women and men have trouble grasping exactly what the other person is saying if it is presented in an emotionally charged manner. It is difficult to stay unaffected in the presence of someone else's strong feelings. One person's agony rubs off on the other. Anger often produces a defensive-aggressive stance in others. This is doubly true in a relationship because people feel responsible for one another. People who are bonded do not easily ignore the other's strong emotions.

"Emotional contagion" is the rule in relationships. For example, if you're feeling depressed, eventually your partner will feel the weight of the depression. Many therapists avoid scheduling deeply depressed patients at the end of the day because it leaves them with a subtle depression of their own. Videos of depressed clients in treatment show the therapist adopting the same slow cadence of speech and depressed posture (just as babies mimic the cadence and voices of their parents).

Concealing Feelings

If sharing your emotions is risky is it better to keep them inside? Concealing feelings is appropriate at times; but people who are sensitive to one another will know something unusual is happening.

Discussing emotions and feelings with the man in your life may prove to be difficult, if not impossible. Suppose you notice that something is going on with him and inquire about it. Don't be surprised if there's a denial. Commonly, people both telegraph their emotions and simultaneously deny their existence to the observer who notices them:

"Are you angry, Bill?"

"No, damn it, why do you ask?"

If Bill denies he has feelings about something, you would be ill-advised to try to prove to him that he's being evasive. Men typically deny their own feelings and give women the message they shouldn't display their feelings either.

If you have taken a verbal beating for being attuned to your partner's emotions you are likely to retreat from such attempts in the future and thereby increase the relational gap. This is how women and men grow apart. It happens subtly and over a long time. Thereafter, when a crisis occurs, a couple has no way to recognize and solve the problem.

Maybe you've noticed a male in your life seems depressed or down and you say, "How are you feeling?" He says, "Fine," and moves on to another subject, in effect denying your perception that he is experiencing something uncomfortable. "Fine" is a dead-end response, followed by a change in the subject to keep the interaction superficial. There is no acknowledgment of your interest or validation of your understanding, whether it's correct or incorrect.

What's to be done when this kind of poor communication pattern is established? Should one give up? Having tried everything you can think of, should you do it all again? Instead, it may take a crisis to break through this pattern.

Timothy and Marla: The Curative Powers of Emotional Crises

While we have said that emotional contagion can be a serious impediment to a relationship, it is also true that sometimes nothing less than a crisis is necessary before a couple can improve their relationship. Usually, people do not *consciously* invite a crisis into their lives.

But, that is not to say that people never "accidentally-deliberately" arrange for one. Calling one's spouse by one's lover's name is one way to bring matters to a head. In any case, if you've been alive long enough, crises will find their way into your existence as it did with Marla and Timothy.

Marla was deeply pessimistic about her marriage during our first session:

"No one can help us. I know our problem is unsolvable. I don't even know why I'm here; it's hopeless. And yet, I can't give up," said Marla, who burst into tears on and off throughout our first session.

Marla's appearance was wholesome, in fact, unusually so. She wore no make-up, her hair was short and slightly curled, brushed away from her face, and her clothes were casual and artless.

Married twenty years, Marla was forty-three and had "gone with" her husband since she was seventeen. "Our marriage," she said, "has not been good for a long time but I've had the fleeting thought—during the few times I've been rational in the last weeks—that this situation is so serious it might bring us closer.

"We've never talked like we are talking now. Timothy is even showing some emotion. In fact, I think this is the first time in our marriage he's shown deep emotion—to the point where he has cried. When he gets emotional, I'm somehow actually relieved."

What was this "unsolvable problem" that was tearing them apart but also bringing them together? Marla tried to place events in some type of chronological order. In December, she'd gone in for her yearly gynecological exam. A week later the doctor called Marla at work to inform her that her lab test came back positive for *herpes*. Because she was at work Marla asked him to call her home later. When the doctor called, he broke the bad news to Timothy but suggested another test was in order to confirm the diagnosis.

Marla, a nurse, frantically reviewed the medical literature and was further horrified to learn that herpes is regarded as a *sexually transmitted disease*. The article did indicate other possible ways of contracting herpes. However, her gynecologist flatly stated to her that herpes was "sexually caused, period!"

Another test was scheduled. Marla and Timothy visited the doctor together to hear the results. He informed them that the second lab test confirmed the diagnosis but assured them that herpes was not life-threatening. It would be painful in its active phase and there was a remote chance of cancer developing at a later date; however, its main consequence was discomfort.

Marla and Timothy had to ask *THE* question again: Could herpes be contracted in some way other than through sex? The doctor insisted herpes is sexually transmitted and that other routes of transmission are rare.

Timothy and Marla stumbled out of the office in a state of agitated shock. Marla said, "I told Timothy, 'how can this be? It's impossible.' Then it dawned on me; Timothy was involved with someone. He vehemently denied any other relationship and was shocked that I even suggested it."

Timothy could not accept the lab result. He phoned the doctor to get more information but was startled by the doctor's accusatory tone: "We know how men are, they like to sleep around. Although you don't want to hear it, herpes is sexually transmitted."

Stunned because he knew he had not had any other sexual partner, Timothy spent the next two hours in a mental frenzy going over his wife's life, searching for clues of her involvement with another man that, in his naivete, he might have ignored. He came to the conclusion that Marla was having an affair. When she got home from work, Marla asked about the news from the doctor.

"Let's take a ride," he said.

Marla asked again, "What did the doctor say?"

Timothy reiterated, "Let's take a ride." Puzzled, curious, but not overly upset, (since this was something they often did to have privacy from the children) Marla changed and out they went.

When they were safely away from the house, Timothy said, "Marla, who are you seeing?"

"Who am I seeing for what?"

She felt as if she couldn't catch her breath. Her heart began pounding as she realized his question was connected to his call to the doctor. She said, "Timothy, what are you talking about?" "One of us has been involved with another person," Timothy said, "and it's not me."

Marla, as she sat hunched over in the office chair said, "We drove around for two hours talking. It took that long for him to settle down and realize I'd not been having an affair. But, two days later when he walked in after work I noticed a funny look on his face. He wouldn't look me in the eye. After dinner the two younger boys went to bed and we went to the bedroom to talk. He accused me of leaving a job in March *not* because of ethical considerations and a poor working environment as I had told him, but because I was trying to break up a serious romance with my lover. He was crazed, loving me and hating me at the same time.

"He had never expressed himself like that before. His main emotion in the past had been anger. At least now he was deeply hurt. But, what a price to pay to find out he cares. I've never seen him like this. He wakes me up in the middle of the night because he's suddenly had a thought—right in his sleep. For example, he recalled that last summer I wasn't as cheerful as usual. Therefore, I must have been having trouble with my affair. He keeps accusing me of doing something I have not done! He's acting ridiculous, but I feel sorry for him; I end up comforting him, making sure he's settled down and feels O.K. It's been going on for six weeks and the bad feelings are as intense as they were on day one. This is ruining our lives."

Marla's plaintiff voice switched to a frustrated tone: "His anger has always been offensive to me. I'm from a home where no one fought. My parents had disagreements but they didn't yell and shout and act like they hated one another. Soon after we were married Timothy began expressing his anger. I would be so hurt I would cry and cry. That continued for two years until I finally got fed up and decided to stand up for myself. From that day to this we have had drag down, drawn out shouting matches. Yet, I hate to fight!

"Now he is obsessed by the situation. However, when he confronts me, his accusations are followed by passionate avowals of love. I haven't adjusted to it. I wonder how he can say the mean things he does. On the one hand it sickens me; on the other, to have Timothy jealous is a new experience. We've known each other since we were seventeen and I've never given him the slightest reason to be concerned or worried about me and other men. When I went to college for a nursing degree I ran to class and ran home to make sure everything was taken care of. When I'm not at work I'm always at home with the children and I'm not flirtatious. I love my husband. I want to scream and yell and pound him as hard as I can, I'm so hurt and angry. And yet I know he's hurting, too, and I feel sad for him.

"Now that he's upset about our medical problem, I feel he's become totally involved with me. He's very passionate, saying things he's never said, like how he can't live without me and that he loves me. He is very excited and interested in *me*, sexually. It's so mixed up, it's weird and crazy. On the one hand, I can't stand the intensity and fear. On the other hand, I feel Timothy and I are focused and really locked together for the first time.

"I'll feel settled, believing everything's talked out and then suddenly he'll flare up again and I'm in despair. I think about divorce, I think about separation. I can't support myself and the boys in any comfort, yet I feel that I can't stand another day of this."

Marla and Timothy's Backgrounds

To better understand what Marla and Timothy are going through and how gender contributes to their difficulties, we should know more about their backgrounds. Remember, they each come by their patterns honestly. No one's to blame.

Timothy

Timothy was raised in an atmosphere of dissension. His parents fought constantly. As he put it, "My parents can't live without fighting." His eldest sister is mentally unstable to the extent that she can't work or be around other people because she verbally and physically attacks others, throwing things, including furniture. According to Timothy, "she becomes a raving maniac."

The way his father and sister act out their emotions has had a subtle but powerful effect on Timothy. Frightened by his sister's sudden rages, Timothy learned to be wary but never aggressive with her. But, his own repressed anger could not be contained indefinitely. He became aggressive toward women and those who were weaker and younger. He learned that the aggressive emotional displays pay off in dominance and that males are allowed to verbalize aggression and hostility while females search for ways to placate them.

Marla

Marla's upbringing was very different. Because her family was "emotionally cool"—no hugs, kisses or overt anger was permitted— emotional displays raised rather than lowered her anxiety level.

Marla felt ignored and emotionally starved as she grew up. The atmosphere at home was flat. If Marla or one of her siblings cried, they were told to "stop it." Any display of exuberance or excited, happy feelings, resulted in the children being told to quiet down. Marla said, "We were a herd of children. Nothing was personal, no one was singled out, and if we talked about ourselves, my parents showed no interest or said we shouldn't talk about ourselves because 'it wasn't becoming.' I never did figure out what that meant."

Marla was programmed to accept the emotional distance that Timothy demanded. She was uncomfortable with it but she'd already learned that women, in particular, had to blend in with the emotional tone of the more powerful males.

In therapy Marla learned that the fights between her and Timothy provided the emotional heat she longed for. The passion and intimacy Marla unconsciously sought were available to her during their angry encounters and in the present crisis. This indirect effort to emotionalize their relationship was evident from the early stages of their marriage.

Marla and Timothy's Early Married Life

Marla and Timothy began dating while Marla was still in high school and went together for six years before marrying. "I don't know if I fell madly in love with Timothy but looking back, I think I loved him. I did know I wanted to marry him and that he'd be a good husband." Marla's dream, like many women's, was to find the "right man": a man who could support the family, a man who would be loyal and true.

Even before the marriage, Marla knew that Timothy had "bad days." She ignored these early episodes because her dreams of marriage and family predominated. On their honeymoon she could no longer deny that Timothy was a moody and demanding person. Her memories of the honeymoon are dominated by his criticism, demands, and his refusal to be sexual with her because she displeased him in some unexpected way.

Marla's response to Timothy's anger was to try to please him as her mother had tried to please her father. She tried to soothe him, serve him, or talk him into feeling good. She never directly confronted him or allowed him to know how hurtful he was. She was afraid to.

Motherhood was the beginning of change in their relationship. "When the babies came, I didn't pamper Timothy as much but I always took care of him, made sure we had meals together and that the kids were as settled as possible. The family sort of danced around him. Sometimes I think I'm *bad* for having focused so much on Timothy instead of the kids, but I can't hold a candle to my mom. She lived for my dad. Probably that's why I'd get so mad at Timothy for being moody. To me, it seems like everything is taken care of for him. He *shouldn't* be that way.

"When he 'hits the door' and starts in on whomever he sees first—usually me—and has a fit about some minor thing like a magazine on a chair, I can't take it any more. I fight back. It is as though he can be any way he wants with us: nasty, cranky, mean. If he doesn't settle down,

I feel put-upon and get really mad and blow up. We fight and then have an evening of silence.

"But, he's always in a reasonable mood by Friday night because he wants sex on the weekend. That makes me mad, too. If he can control himself when he wants sex, why can't he be decent at other times?"

As the years went by, Marla and Timothy's relationship remained static. They were locked into old emotional habits. Most of the time Marla walked around angry or indifferent to Timothy. That was her defense against the hurt she felt at not having a mate who treated her with kindness and civility. He continued his efforts to dominate through emotional tyranny but got less back for his efforts. Eventually, they reached an unpleasant accommodation with one another.

A Positive Response To The Crisis

Ironically, after the doctor had been so insistent that herpes was not only the correct diagnosis but that the disease had been sexually transmitted, one morning he called Marla somewhat sheepishly: The lab he had been using had been making mistakes in their tests. He recommended she be retested. She was, and the *result was negative!*

Both of them were furious with the lab and the doctor but when that calmed down, they were still left with the worsening problems in their relationship. It would have been preferable had they each simultaneously taken responsibility for changing their feelings and behavior. But, real life seldom works so smoothly and fairly.

Once in therapy, it was Marla who was most willing to make changes. Since it was in Marla's self-interest to avoid the destructive experience she was having with her own anger, she was willing to find new outlets for her distress.

In response to Timothy's angry feelings, Marla learned to maintain her composure and respond by saying things like, "I'll consider what you're trying to say but I can't understand you when you're shouting and carrying on. It offends me. I'll talk to you about it but first you have to stop shouting."

Initially, Timothy mocked her new stance and redoubled his efforts to reengage her in the game of "rule through angry emotions." She consistently ignored this invitation to fight. She held her ground and left Timothy no choice but to cook in his own anger or play by new rules.

Old habits die hard. He used withdrawal when anger failed. But, this distancing deprived him of the interaction he needed so he eventually had to call a truce. She agreed, if he would agree to work on their problems in therapy.

Once they each understood that they were programmed to act in certain ways as women and men as well as how their early development had generated needs they were trying to satisfy in dysfunctional ways, they were open to change.

Marla and Timothy's Responses To Therapy

The therapy itself was long and complicated. In essence, this is what took place: Timothy and Marla came to an agreement that they had a problem they were both responsible for, and if they didn't solve it, the marriage would dissolve.

We utilized a Gender Sensitive No-Fault approach. Rather than determining who was to blame for what, we refocused on how they were acting out the male and female roles they had learned in their respective families. Marla understood that she tolerated and thereby encouraged Timothy's anger by trying to calm him in the early years of their relationship.

After the birth of their child, she began fighting with him on his terms—it was insult for insult. While she had an underlying need for closeness and deeply felt its absence, she nevertheless accommodated herself to a distant relationship. After all, she'd learned to do this as a little girl in her own family.

Timothy was very depressed when he was able to admit that his life had been so profoundly shaped by his aggressive father and his out-of-control sister. He was horrified to discover he'd so identified with these two models in his childhood that he sought out a woman whom he could similarly terrorize and that it would extend to his own children.

Thereafter, this couple had many successes (with the inevitable reversals) as they forged new patterns. Timothy learned that men could express their love through sex but that sex could also be used to control others in an aggressive way. He was now able to surface his repressed emotions by channeling his sexual expressions into his feelings of love and tenderness. Marla responded very positively to this change and became more available for lovemaking. It took her a while to understand that sex need not be exploitative.

Marla experienced some anger when she understood she'd modeled her own life on her parents' behavior and that her mother had led her to deny her own needs and to serve those of men. This realization also gave her a choice: she could continue to live by the old rules or develop new ones.

Thereafter, when she caught herself giving in to Timothy because it was easier to comply than to battle and suffer the guilt, she would evaluate her own behavior and correct it. They agreed that Timothy was to be reminded when he was bullying her; in turn, she asked Timothy to tell her when she resorted to distancing or pleasing.

Marla not only felt closer to Timothy once his anger diminished, she was more loving and attentive. This in turn fulfilled Timothy's needs. He reciprocated with loving feelings and appreciation for the special care he received from Marla.

While we can't say Marla and Timothy lived happily ever after, they were living happily together when we saw them last. Most importantly, they'd confronted a problem and prevailed. That gave them confidence for the future.

A Practical Guide to Deal with Emotional Differences Between Women and Men

We have learned from reviewing Marla and Timothy's difficulties that many forces were operating in each of their lives and that they brought many of their problems to the marriage. Marla could have insisted Timothy change before she would make an effort to modify her behavior. For purposes of argument, let's suppose that "Timothy was wrong and should change."

What looks like Marla's advantage—that Timothy is to blame and must change—actually puts him in control of Marla's fate; *He* must do something before *she* can benefit.

Instead, Marla decided to alter her behavior with the realization that marriage partners make up a system. If one person changes, the system changes. The ultimate effect may be positive, neutral or negative. She was willing to take the chance. This gave her control of her own fate and the marriage than had she insisted that Timothy make the first move.

The closer the attachment and connection between people the greater the opportunity for significant emotional responses and feelings. Therefore, the people you love the most can extract the greatest toll from you. It is also true that they can provide you with some of your greatest satisfactions.

It is extremely important for you to understand that if you are in a position to make changes—even though you are in the habit of

thinking that the person "to blame" should be the one to make the concessions—you are likelier to get what you want if you evaluate and modify yourself. If it results in a better relationship, all the better.

How To Change

Change is My Own Responsibility

"I can change *my* understanding, *my* reactions to others, *my* interactions with others, and *my* behavior. I cannot change other people. The less dependent the solution to my problem depends on forces other than those within my control, the greater the likelihood of success."

One of our most natural and frequent defenses against anxiety or loss of self-esteem is to blame others. Since we are social animals, there is always someone close to us to blame. If, for some reason, this won't do, we externalize by blaming the people next door, those of another race or religion, "foreigners," or "fate."

Actually, externalizing can be a good defensive practice. It keeps people from feeling terrible about themselves. Nevertheless, the upshot of blame is that interpersonal problems are not solved. The accused person is dedicated to their own beliefs and when they experience your effort to cast responsibility upon them, they shore up their own defenses. Usually, the criticism is returned a hundred fold. This is especially true when the message is delivered in highly emotional tones. Result: Stalemate.

If you can only be happy when something or someone remote from you must changed, you are destined for disappointment. For example, if you can never rest or be happy as long as one person in this world is going hungry, then you will never be happy or satisfied. If the economic system of the world must become capitalistic or communistic or socialistic before your world is O.K., be prepared for a long wait because you have no personal control over such things.

At this point you might protest that your husband, lover, or someone with whom you have pledged to share your fate, is hardly on the same plane as poverty or economic systems. True, but this does not mean because the person you have in mind is socially, physically or emotionally close to you, they are going to be responsive to your *need* that they change. If you need emotional closeness from your mate and he is emotionally cool, you may have to accept that as a fact of life.

I am the Starting Point for Change

One of our great accomplishments as human beings is that we develop a *self*; and this self and its organization (personality) are relatively constant. The self gives us an identity and the foundation for a social identity. We recognize ourselves and others recognize us too. If we make significant changes, people around us try to bring us into line because their psychological and social lives depend upon our *predictability.* If we change, we disturb their expectations and they try to bring us back into line or avoid us. Consequently, we have to deal with other people's reactions as well as our own resistance.

Anyone that ever tried to change some habit or way of thinking can testify that even *self-control* is difficult. Have you ever been on a diet? Do you now consider it a success? Have you regained your original weight and then some? Because we have so much resistance to changing ourselves, we prefer to have the other person change—it's easier.

You will undertake one of the most difficult tasks in life if you try to change the gender-related behavior of another person—given the fact that gender is one of the deepest aspects of our identity. You will be more successful in fulfilling your needs if you try to *understand* others and focus on dimensions of your own life that *can be* modified.

Rules for Understanding The Other Person's Behavior and Changing Your Own.

1. **Gender conceit** is bred in from birth. Families and cultures train females and males to think about and react to emotions differently. Accept the fact that you must make changes in your expectations of males. If not, you are setting yourself up for disappointment

based on gender conceit: You feel your way is the right way, the unquestioned way. In fact, your way is natural to you and it's different—but it is not *the only way or the right way.*

2. Do not **gunnysack**, i.e., store up your complaints until you're overwhelmed by anger and hurt. Getting into a rage may give you the courage to abandon your passive stance but you'll do your interests more harm than good. A highly emotional and aggressive display eclipses the real issue(s). He may respond by ridiculing you, or he might feel so guilty or eager to stop the display that he gives in, promising to "be better." Do not expect promises extracted by these means to be kept.

3. **Verbalize your thoughts and feelings** as close to the time that they are generated as you can. If you don't express yourself, there will be no chance of change and your anger and disappointment will reduce the quality of your life. When something bothers you about the other person, make it a principle to bring it to his attention and persist in having the issue heard before you reach the boiling point.

4. If you cannot reach a satisfactory **mutual understanding**, set your own course of action. For example: Mary works hard and loves to do things on weekends. Marty, her husband, also works hard, but he sees the weekend as a time to "kick back," do things with his buddies, work on his hobby or hang around the house.

If discussion fails to remedy this difference, Mary should plan something enjoyable on the weekend that she can do by herself or with others. In this way Marty will get what he needs and Mary enjoys herself. We can anticipate that both Marty and Mary will find ways to spend weekend time with one another because they each want to, not because Mary complains.

5. *A man is not your "mother"* and you're not a baby; he does not know what you are feeling. You have to tell him. If your response is either that you have told him and he doesn't listen or that he should know or it isn't worth telling him, you are in a no win situation. Once you clearly tell someone what you want or don't want they have the option of complying or not.

But, if you don't make your wishes clear the likelihood of having them fulfilled drops to near zero (with a simultaneous rise in your frustration). You may not have your needs met no matter how clearly you communicate them so it takes a certain amount of courage just to find this out.

6. Men tend to limit themselves to what is pragmatic and logical, avoiding the emotional. **If you want to be heard, you have to learn his language.** If you encounter someone who does not speak your language, how far would you get shouting or screaming at them? Not only would they not understand you, they'd turn you off. Women say, "Men should be more emotionally in tune with me!" Maybe so, but they are not. Work toward your goal but don't bet your life or relationship on it.

Summary

Please note: the emphasis in this chapter is not about how women can change men; it is about understanding the emotional differences between women and men, and then doing what is possible to deal with these differences.

As therapists we highly recommend that men join a male *consciousness raising* group. These groups help men to "get in touch with themselves." When men are given the green light by other men to express their emotions, they are *released from the strict male code that feelings are to be repressed* if one is to remain a male in good standing. This comfort with emotions can then be carried over to a man's relationships with his wife and children.

The ideas for change listed above, in combination with individual attention to the details and particulars of your life, are some of the important tools you need to improve your life. Remember, *when one person in a system changes, the other will necessarily respond in some way.*

The next chapter deals with the profound though subtle differences in the sexual make-up of women and men and how these differences affect relationships. With this knowledge in hand, you will be in a position to significantly improve your love life.

3

SEXUAL DIFFERENCES AND SIMILARITIES

Q: Why did God create Adam and Eve naked?
A: So they could air their differences.

During the first two years of their marriage Donna found sex interesting and pleasurable. It was a different story after their son was born. Keith, 28, was constantly after her for sex. In turn, Donna, 25, felt harassed, inadequate, guilty, and turned off. It seemed to her that Keith was insisting on sex at times when she had neither the interest nor the time for it.

Working full-time in a family business with Keith and caring for her son left Donna exhausted. She felt guilty about not fulfilling Keith's "needs" but when he persisted and was sexually aggressive, she felt he was selfishly ignoring her as a person. She began to resent him and withdraw.

Keith was feeling frustrated and angry because his dream about marriage—including the idea that sex would be plentiful—was becoming a nightmare. When Donna occasionally agreed to make love he was still disappointed because he detected it was out of a sense of obligation; there was no passion. To retaliate, he wanted to ignore her, to show her how it felt. However, he could never endure long enough "to teach her a lesson."

Donna was not immune to his subtle attacks. When
she felt she could no longer tolerate her situation she
consulted a psychiatrist. He suggested a *paradoxical*
approach to her problem. This treatment plan called for
her to turn the tables on Keith by insisting on more sex
than he could stomach. Specifically, Donna was to offer
Keith sex several times each day. If he faltered, she was
to beg him for sex, even demand it.

Keith was disturbed by her sudden change of
behavior but having his needs met was exciting and
pleasurable—for the first two days. As one might
imagine, he soon tired of her pursuit and began to refuse
Donna's overtures no matter how demanding she was.

The good news is this approach stopped
Keith's constant harassment of his wife for sex;
the bad news is that it did nothing toward
working through the underlying issues
between them. He was befuddled and
frightened by her aggressive behavior but he
wasn't fooled by her demands. He didn't
mistake Donna's sexual overtures for genuine
interest in improving their sexual relationship.
He eventually filed for divorce. Donna greeted
Keith's action with a sigh of relief: She was
through with the marriage.

While Donna and Keith's approach to solving
their problem is unusual, sexual incompatibility
and difficulties in discussing sexual issues are
common between females and males. Couples
find sex a delicate subject and tend to avoid
talking about it, whether in therapy or in their
daily lives.

Part of this reluctance is a carry over from
being socialized not to discuss sex, especially
with *the opposite* sex. Part is due to the hard

lessons people learn when they try to discuss "delicate subjects" that threaten the other person's self-esteem.

Here's another example of the problems which inhibit sexual discussion:

> Edith, married for twenty-four years, had difficulty communicating about sex with her husband. In their second year of marriage she wanted to share one of her sexual fantasies with him. She thought she would ease into the discussion by asking him, "Do you ever have sexual fantasies?" He quickly squelched the subject. He regarded talking about his innermost, forbidden thoughts as too dangerous.

> Edith immediately decided she must be abnormal; she never brought the subject up again until she was in the midst of divorce counseling. In the meantime, their relationship had unnecessarily deteriorated.

Can We Talk? Probably Not!

Although sexual desire is a powerful force that brings men and women together, it paradoxically creates barriers between them. Once there's a union, more than pure desire is needed to create a healthy and lasting relationship. When there's "trouble in paradise," why don't people talk these matters out?

Easier said than done. Couples have great difficulty in discussing sex frankly. What causes this problem? Males learn to focus on sex, think about sexual pleasure, and desire sex earlier than do females. They aggressively seek or deeply desire sex. They discuss sex openly with other males. They buy magazines and look at videos that depict explicit sex. Simultaneously, women have been trained to be cautious about explicit sexually thoughts and actions.

Girls and young women are supposed to avoid having sex and to be passive if they engage in it. A sexually aggressive girl is a "bad" girl. She is certainly not supposed to pursue sexual "conquests." Instead, she learns to think of herself as sexual prey and to fear the physical and social consequences of "illicit" (unmarried) sex.

She's the one who will become pregnant and be responsible for the child; she's the one who will be sterilized—or worse—by venereal diseases; she's the one who will lose her reputation and standing if *her* sexuality is publicized. The prostitutes go to jail while the johns go back home! The police bring the women to justice and ignore their customers.

Inundated as we are with suggestive sexual words and pictures by way of TV, art, magazine advertisements, articles, movies, and novels, sex should be an easy topic for women and men to discuss. Nevertheless, sex is usually not openly discussed even in marital relationships. So much of a person's identity is based on their gender and so much of gender is involved with sex that sexual matters—for both women and men—become a very difficult subject.

Different Meanings of Sex to Men and Women

Sexual stresses between women and men are compounded by the different meanings sex has for them:

1. Women view sex as *flowing from* an intimate emotional relationship whereas men use sex *to express* intimacy. Women want to be in love to have sex; men want to have sex to express their love.

2. Women want love, a commitment, emotional closeness and an intimate relationship that eventually includes sex; males seek intercourse and sexual play with variety and adventure. For men, sex and love will eventually be combined in a committed relationship.

3. Women think men place too much importance on physical sex and too little on intimacy. Men at times express intimacy through sex but they also use sex exploitatively. This confuses women. Are they being taken advantage of or loved? (Talking about it might help.)

Although most individuals are somewhat aware of these personal and cultural differences in male and female sexuality, they have great difficulty in applying what they know to their own lives. In marital counseling, where a discussion of sexual problems is often

part of the therapeutic agenda, couples feel shy
and embarrassed when asked to openly and
honestly discuss their sex life.

Doug and Cindy are both 29 years old. They courted
for ten months and have been married four years. Doug
is a hospital administrator and Cindy had just begun her
career as interior decorator when Cindy decided they
needed marriage counseling.
Cindy could no longer cope with Doug's
dissatisfaction with their sex life. There were a few other
"minor difficulties" in their relationship but their main
problem was that Doug wanted and needed sex more
frequently than Cindy. Cindy wanted Doug to be happy
in every way but could not bring herself to make love
with him as often as he wanted. When they did have sex,
both of them agreed it was enjoyable. Cindy usually had
an orgasm and Doug always felt satisfied.
Doug was confused by their courtship; then they'd
made love on a daily basis. What he did not understand,
until it came out in counseling, was that she gave in to
his persistent requests for sex during the courtship
because she loved him so much, not because she desired
sex as often as he did. For Cindy, the courtship was a
romantic interlude which included sexual excitement.
She described that period as "an altered state."
Shortly after the marriage, she returned to her own
steady state. They settled into a twice-a-month sexual
routine that completely baffled and angered Doug. What
he didn't suspect was that even twice a month was once
too often for Cindy. Cindy believed she had an
obligation as a marital partner to provide sex so she
added an extra session of intercourse to fulfill her duty.
Doug never adjusted to this routine. He said, with
annoyance, "I'm afraid to make any romantic moves or
even mention I'm interested in sex because I'll be
rejected. That hurts like hell. We also get into long,
painful discussions about why she either won't, can't or

shouldn't have to have sex when she doesn't want to. Then I have to explain to her again why I need to have more lovemaking. I agree with her, in principle: A person should not be required to have sex when they're not interested. But an angry feeling builds up inside me that I can't control. I feel like I'm trapped with no escape, no outlet."

Cindy's experience was quite different: "I do enjoy sex—occasionally. We do it a lot more often than he says we do. [Here they engaged in an unproductive argument about how many times in the past few months they'd actually had sex.] It never comes to my mind to press Doug about sex and I don't know why he keeps after me when he knows I'm not interested. He makes me feel guilty. Then the only way sex is on my mind is in a negative way. I worry that he'll bug me about sex or give me 'signals' and I'll have to refuse him, which I hate to do.

"I can't understand why he can't get it into his mind to have sex once in a while and not make such a big deal out of it. It doesn't make sense to me. I know men are supposedly more sexual than women but does that mean men should have sex any time they want it? Meanwhile, if I don't want sex, am I supposed to participate anyway? There are many things I want but don't get, so why does he think he should have everything he wants?"

Although they had discussed the same issue repeatedly, neither could understand or meet the other's needs. Yet, Doug and Cindy consider themselves to be reasonable people. They've talked things out and tried to understand one another's point of view. Generally, they succeed but they couldn't straighten out their sex life.

As Cindy's interest in sex nearly disappeared because of the strain it caused, Doug felt Cindy no longer cared about him. To him, sex was a measure of her love for him. Sex represented something Doug needed and when he did not "get lucky," he translated this into rejection, not being loved, and a betrayal.

No matter how often Cindy reassured him that she loved him, he could not abandon the formula: "No sex = no love." There is a manipulative force in the formula because it is unconsciously designed to get Doug what he wants while ignoring his wife's view. "No sex means you don't love me" aroused Cindy's guilt. Eventually she'd give in to Doug to get rid of the feeling that she "should" have sex to be a good wife. On the heels of giving in came anger with both herself and Doug.

Doug and Cindy both asked the question: "Am I the bad one; is something wrong with me?" *Gender Sensitive No-Fault Therapy* takes the position that, "There are no villains; there are differences that need to be understood and used to improve the relationship."

Sexual Differences and Misunderstandings

Doug's interest in and perceived need for sex is the norm for young men. When one person's sexual interest becomes so intense he/she cannot understand the other's feelings and needs, there is bound to be trouble.

In *Roseanne: My Life As A Woman,* an autobiography by Roseanne Barr, Barr describes her first fiancee who "refused to incessantly rut away his life with me, and kept foolishly insisting there were other things to life. He wanted to have separation with me, and I wanted to get closer and closer. You know how men are" (p. 110).

In Barr we find the unusual woman who wants to use sex to get close but runs up against the male need to maintain distance. Some women are sexually aggressive whereas, in our society, men are likelier to regard sex as a desirable and pleasurable experience and to think about sex many times a day.

In contrast, women may not have one overt sexual thought during a day or a week while still desiring closeness, hugging, cuddling, and kissing. This confounds and confuses both sexes. Women don't understand why, when they want to cuddle, men take this to mean they want sex. Men become confused and infuriated when they perceive an invitation for sex which turns out to be "nothing more than hugging."

The confusion about male and female sexuality is demonstrated by those who promote the idea that a woman has the right to pet as heavily as she wants while retaining the right to say, "no." Legally and morally this is an absolutely sound position. Women should be able to say no and have their wish respected.

In the "real world," this is a dangerous policy to advocate because men march to a different drummer. They are more quickly aroused, believe that women say no when they mean maybe or yes, have impaired judgment when sexually stimulated, and are physically able to overpower (rape) a woman. Therefore, differences between the sexes—shorn of politics and moral correctness—need to be taken into account by both women and men. Is there really a difference in sexual desire between women and men?

In 1984, a syndicated advice columnist asked her readers, "Would you be content to be held close and treated tenderly and forget about the 'act'?" Within two weeks 90,000 women replied with 72 percent preferring no sex. A stunning 40 percent of the "no sex" respondents were under forty years of age! (While this isn't a scientific poll, the huge number of replies carry some weight.)

Ironically, if women put themselves into a position to get what they want—holding and cuddling—they also find it is difficult to avoid what they do *not* want: An assumption that tenderness is the low road to intercourse.

When women tell men they desire the warmth and loving feeling of being held and soothed but this is not to be considered foreplay, it seems to incomprehensible to the male. Therefore, if women want to kiss, hug or pet without making love, they must be *assertive* about saying "no." Men misread women's signals then complain about being "led on."

Many women learn to do without kissing and holding, because they learn that such behavior means intercourse to men. These differences in sexual patterns promote problems both in and out of the bedroom. To deal effectively with these differences between the sexes, we need to know more about sex and biology.

Biological Factors

In sexual functioning, women and men are more similar than they are different. But, in practice, the differences are significant. Masters and Johnson's research in the 1960's established that the *sexual response cycles* of women and men are similar. A full sexual experience consists of four distinguishable stages:

1. *Excitement*
2. *Plateau*
3. *Orgasm*
4. *Resolution*

Both men and women experience these phases but they do so at different rates and with varying intensities. These "small differences" become very significant in actual practice. Exploring the similarities and differences in sexual functioning will help us understand *why women and men have trouble getting along.*

1. The **excitement** phase. Males rapidly become excited. Little stimulation is needed for the erection of the penis. For women, excitement usually takes longer than it does for men to be physically and psychologically prepared for intercourse. But five to twenty (or more) minutes can make a big difference to sexual partners. A man who is instantly ready for sex and doesn't allow for a woman's slower arousal cycle will be a

poor lover. Neither of them will reach maximum physical and emotional satisfaction.

2. The **plateau** stage, characterized by a high level of excitement and pleasure, is a different experience for women than men. Once a male reaches this level of excitement he will press on to orgasm. Females who reach the plateau phase have shown three patterns: a. They drop down quickly from plateau to resolution before reaching orgasm; b. They maintain the plateau for a long period and then go to resolution without orgasm; or c. They may go from plateau to orgasm one or more times before resolution. Women can either maintain their excitement far longer than males, they can become excited and skip the orgasm, or they can have multiple orgasms. Female orgasm is unlikely if the male proceeds rapidly from excitement to plateau to orgasm.

3. **Orgasm** for the male involves regular contractions of the penis, rapid heartbeat and breathing, sweating, ejaculation, and other changes. Females have a broader range of responses that include contractions of varying intensities of the first one-third of the vagina and of the uterus and rectal sphincters. Rapid heartbeat, higher blood pressure, nipple erection, sexual flush, and other changes accompany their orgasms.

4. **Resolution** consists of the return to an unexcited sexual stage. This changes rapidly in men but at varying rates for women. Some women can be re-stimulated into another sexual cycle during this phase, whereas men typically must wait between orgasms. Misunderstandings between sexual partners are quite common at this stage of the sexual cycle. If the female is unsatisfied, she may find the male's rapid decline in sexual interest highly frustrating. She may interpret his behavior during resolution as selfishness. Attempts to re-stimulate him soon after orgasm will probably meet with failure, whereas the woman is more readily interested in more lovemaking.

While the sexual response cycle is similar for women and men, the differences that exist are likely to create sexual difficulties for them if they are not understood and managed. Consider how these differences affected the lives of Nadine and Jack:

> Nadine complained bitterly about Jack's pattern of making love with her. After his orgasm he would turn over and fall asleep. Post-coital sleep is a normal response for the male. The female has a slower resolution, called an "afterglow," and she is often confused and hurt about being "abandoned" after the sexual act.
>
> Nadine and Jack were encouraged to talk about their separate perceptions and experiences. Understanding these differences allowed them to manage their love-making. Sex is such a taboo subject that couples often need encouragement and a safe setting to voice their concerns and discuss mutually agreeable sex.

When Nadine understood that Jack's natural physiological processes were different from hers, she was no longer angry or hurt. They both learned that his post-coital slumber was as pleasant and natural for him as her afterglow was for her.

Jack learned to tell Nadine how wonderful their love-making was and inform her that he was going to "nod off" in the warmth of her love. Upon awakening, he wanted to talk with her about his experience and about things in general. She was able to accommodate his pattern, and settled into her own afterglow, thinking her own thoughts.

Other efforts to understand male–female differences in sexuality are based on evolutionary theory. Anthropologist Donald Symons (1979, p. 150) believes:

> There is a female human nature and a male human nature, and these natures are extraordinarily different.... Men and women differ in their sexual natures because throughout the immensely long hunting and gathering phase of human evolutionary history the sexual desires and dispositions that were adaptive for either sex were, for the other, tickets to reproductive oblivion.

Symons believes variety is built into the male psyche and that male humans, like male animals, tire of copulating with one female and become immediately interested if another is available. The female animal doesn't seem to care about variety. [He's in error about this; some species show female patterns of multiple partner copulation.] Symons postulates that the human male is visually orientated and is naturally aroused at the mere sight of an attractive woman. Men, serially stimulated by the sight and presence of many women, would be sexually promiscuous throughout their lives if there was no social regulation of their behavior.

Women, according to Symons, look for quality, not quantity. They pick the male who will be the fittest possible father for their children; one who has promise as a provider. He believes women lack sexual wanderlust and do not have the innate taste for variety that men do: "Women do not generally seem to experience a pervasive, autonomous desire for men to whom they are not married.... A woman is likeliest to experience a wish for extramarital sex when she perceives another man as somehow superior to her husband or when she is in some way dissatisfied with her marriage."

Studies of male and female extramarital affairs could be construed to support Symon's argument: Men more often than women are involved in extramarital sexual relationships. What Symons did not consider is the discriminatory nature of societies; custom and laws, of not nature, are aligned against female *promiscuity*. This is especially evident in "primitive" cultures. If women break their marital vows they are severely stigmatized, even killed. No such culturally dictated fate awaits unfaithful husbands in any known society. The double standard is widespread.

A Texas statute made it a crime for a wife to kill her husband's lover if she discovered them having sex but the husband had a right to kill his wife's lover if he caught them. This legal bias may have something to do with the more frequent violation of sexual codes by men and the fact that they make laws that sanctify their behaviors.

There is ample evidence that as women increasingly move into the work place, gain more independence and find opportunities to have affairs, they are doing so at an increasing rate. While they have not caught up with male extra-marital rates (about 70 percent), 25 percent to 30 percent of married women now admit to being "unfaithful."

Sorting out which of the differences between the sexes are due to culture and which are physiologically determined is a difficult, if not impossible task. The most important issue in female—male relations is *how people perceive themselves and others.* Self-report studies are revealing.

Do Men And Women See Themselves As Sexually Similar Or Different?

The pioneering Kinsey reports (1950s) found that men and women gave markedly different responses to erotic materials. About four times as many men as women said they were "turned on" by erotic and pornographic materials. What aroused women more than men were the love themes in romantic but non-pornographic movies.

More recent self-report studies suggest that women and men seem to be more alike than different in their *physiological arousal* patterns to erotic materials. Julia Heiman (1980) investigated the possibility that women might be less likely than men to report their actual reactions to sexual material.

To get past this self-reporting bias she equipped male college students with strain gauges (placed around the base of the penis) to measure erections. She equipped the women with a device that detected vaginal changes indicating sexual arousal. The college students then listened to three types of erotic and romantic tapes in various combinations along with one that was sexually neutral.

Heiman found there were *no significant differences* in men's and women's physiological rates of sexual response to these materials. While women may be as *physically* responsive to sexual material as men, the difference is they do not identify their reactions as erotic arousal. We infer that women are trained to ignore or dismiss these sexual cues or sexual cues are less available to their consciousness.

Based purely on biological factors women and men are well suited to one another. If both women and men are sexually responsive to erotic materials, why do they have so many problems with each other over matters relating to sex?

Cultural Variables In Getting The Sexes Together

We've seen how people get into difficulties about sex when it would seem that sexual

sharing should be one of the pleasurable and
bonding forces in a relationship. Some of these
differences between the sexes are genetically
programmed and some are cultural and/or
individual.

Every known culture dictates different
paths for men and women. By adolescence or
early adulthood, when the two sexes are
preparing to close the social and psychological
gaps that began with childhood, they are ill-
prepared to be sensitive and reciprocal to each
other's social, emotional and sexual needs.

Adolescence and young adulthood are
periods when young women and men have to
find new ways of being together. They come to
this task of integrating their lives with
markedly different perspectives: She wants
love, commitment, and a relationship; he
wants sex, variety, freedom, autonomy and
adventure. ("Commitment" is a concept that
can scare otherwise courageous males into
headlong flight!)

Cultural influences are responsible for many
of the differences in male and female sexuality.
Our society encourages and allows men to be
relatively free sexually, to be aggressive and to
regard their dominant position as natural.
Males are encouraged to be aware of their
sexual urges and to get them satisfied as soon
and as often as possible.

One of our friends has a humorous way of
characterizing the male orientation toward sex:

> The difference between men, women, and sex, is
> that special male affliction, GONADAL PSYCHOSIS.
> When a male is sexually aroused, the blood necessary to

erect his penis is taken from the brain. It is replaced by semen so that the brain can continue to function—after a fashion. Since semen is well-known for its inability to carry oxygen, rational thinking is impossible. As the brain can only function for a short period with semen, it directs the body to seek instant relief from the sexual build–up.

If the tension is not released, the male whines, he begs, his feelings are hurt, his hostility goes up and his self-esteem declines to a dangerous level. Any woman, i.e., a SDU—Sperm Depository Unit—not interested in a brain-drain session becomes THE ENEMY. She can expect pouting, withdrawal, and overt or covert anger.

According to this formula, it is understandable that a female experiences guilt, a feeling of responsibility and a need to submit to sex. She simply does not understand that males are like a diabetic who needs insulin. Similar to an alcoholic or anyone else with an addiction, a male in the throes of "gonadal psychosis" cannot be dealt with by rational means.

Women often have difficulty understanding men's need for sex. Men are equally unskilled at empathizing with the more subtle emotional-sexual processes of women. Men complain about not getting enough sex, seeing it as withholding behavior by the woman whom they want to love. Women are disturbed because men want sex without regard to their wishes and moods. Men seemingly treat sex as something apart from the rest of the flow of life whereas women include sex with a variety of other considerations: security, sensitivity, reliability, thoughtfulness, etc.

A further mischief-maker in male/female relationships is the natural tendency for individuals to believe the other person's views of sex are the same as their own. Women and men both feel *their* natural impulses or rhythms are right but the other person's are foreign. They arrive at this position mainly because they have been socialized differently.

Different Paths of Male and Female Sexual Socialization

Let us review: 1. How females and males acquire their particular brands of sexuality; 2. How these differences are refined in adolescence; 3. How (1) and (2) influence adult lovemaking.

Early Development

There is a biological basis for some sexual differences. Males on the average are taller, heavier, and have a greater ratio of muscle to fat than females. Because the male embryo is genetically programmed to produce testosterone, boys become more active and aggressive than girls. In any contest based on strength, especially upper body strength, males usually prevail.

However, this muscular advantage should not lead to the conclusion that male aggressiveness could not be channeled into non-violent forms or be deprogrammed. Indeed, male and female roles could be reversed; boys would be comparatively passive and girls aggressive. Nevertheless, male dominance is now institutionalized. It has been passed on from one generation to another and is deeply imbedded in a wide variety of cultures. There are few, if any, exceptions. The gendering process starts early. By the age of twenty-seven months, almost all children learn to which sexual category people belong. We refer to this developmental achievement as *gender identification*.

Sex role refers to separate social prescriptions for female and male behavior, thoughts, and feelings. These roles are probably learned at an earlier age than we can detect with present methods. Anne Campbell's book, *The Opposite Sex* (1989) cites research showing that in families with children of different sexes, girls spontaneously pair up with girls, and boys with boys. Even children of *ten months* show preferences for same-sex children. One year-olds prefer to observe children of their own sex. They are not fooled by differences in clothing. They can tell the difference by the way the other child walks!

While children have some inborn gender tendencies, culture, socialization, and learning are also important factors in determining behavior. How does this happen?

Males and females form bonds with their primary caretaker, usually the mother. Females, because of their gender, can forever maintain these close bonds with mothers and model their behavior accordingly. Women do not have to *reject* the original love object

(mother) to become feminine. How are they to
learn about males? Indirectly!

The male is programmed to reject his
mother as a role model and to identify with his
father and other males. We know boys can
develop male identity without the father
because playmates, neighbors, the media, and
other influences will encourage the male into a
masculine identity. But, sons lost something
when their fathers left the home to participate
in the industrial world—so did daughters. Now
their mothers too are leaving the home in
greater numbers.

For boys, failing to make a switch from
identification with mother to masculinity leads
to severe punishment. Psychoanalysts and
others who study human development call
attention to the lasting effect on males of their
necessary rejection of the original love and
identification figure, the mother. To be male
means, above all, to *avoid any female qualities*!
Once the male takes the masculine path, his
potential empathy for women will decrease.

When males and females get together as
women and men later in life they should not be
surprised to find a mysterious distance
between them. Many of our female clients
complain bitterly that no matter how hard they
try to establish closeness with men, they fail.

Women would not be so frustrated if they
understood the closeness they experienced
with their mothers can rarely be attained with
men. A woman's frustration is based on the fact
that a man is forced to reject his identification
with mother and develop a separate identity

thereby losing a certain amount of empathy with women.

Adolescent Sexuality

Let us now consider how adolescents develop socially and sexually, and the consequences of their separate perspectives and experiences.

Bernstein and Warner, in *Women Treating Women* (1984) write, "Usually girls, in contrast to boys, start self-stimulation later and are less vigorous, less focused, stimulate themselves with less frequency and show less self-absorption.... They are more vague about their anatomy than boys. This is true visually, tactilely and in naming of genital parts" (p. 18).

This behavior contrasts sharply with the male, whose genitals are more readily available to his sight and touch. Most adolescent males, but not females, masturbate to orgasm. Females are admonished not to touch themselves and are subtly or directly discouraged from identifying, exploring or expressing their sexuality. The language they learn to identify their sex organs is itself vague. "The vagina" is used as a global term rather than to identify a particular structure.

Adolescent girls feel self-conscious about their body and worry their breasts are too big or too small; some girls hunch their shoulders to hide their new womanly shape. Developing physical sexuality may be exaggerated with tight, "temptress" clothes or outfits that totally hide the frightening new body within.

For girls, budding sexuality is often perceived as a loss of control and mastery over their bodies. Males, in contrast, are encouraged to use their bodies as expressions of power and incorporate sex as a part of that experience. Adolescent boys eagerly seek sexual outlets as their hormones and peers urge them on.

What adolescents have in common is that each sex wants to be involved with the other. However, their reasoning and motivation differ. Girls want male attention. This means to date, find a boyfriend and to develop a quality relationship. Boys are more interested in a physical than an emotional relationship. They see their task as obtaining sex without lasting responsibility or the compromise of their freedom and future.

A girl's wish for a boyfriend does not necessarily stimulate her sexual urges. Her overwhelming wishes are to be close, to have a boyfriend, the pleasure of his company, and to kiss and hug. Whereas the adolescent male consciously seeks sexual outlets, the female looks for affiliation and emotional closeness. The sexual component of the relationship is vague to her. She rarely looks for a "male pelt" to hang on her belt.

Boys are eager to see the female figure, naked, preferably. Girls often react with disgust when they see male genitalia; they are eager to explore relationships, not to become sexual for sex itself.

The Sexual Experience: Different for Men and Women

Sex play and intercourse have different meanings for young men and women. Males are likelier to seek out females so they can experience sex whereas females are likelier to submit to sex so they can have a relationship. You will seldom find a girl pressuring a male for an introduction to the sexual world while boys relentlessly pursue girls for sex. Girls who want boyfriends have to deal with male pressures to engage in sex. They soon learn that many males require sex if there is to be any relationship.

Men are more definite about their sexual desires and needs than are women. This drives them to seek out females and to find a way to move quickly into sex. Females want to be with men, get to know them, and be lovingly caressed. They are frightened and irritated by male's sexual pushiness and consider it dehumanizing. Females are in a predicament because they fear loss of a relationship if they do not submit.

Most girls begin as reluctant participants in sex. Whatever their expectations of sex are, they usually experience some significant disappointments.

It lasted only two months but it was long enough to turn Janet's world upside down. A shy ninth grader, Janet had never had a boyfriend or a friendship with a boy, so when a male senior showed an interest in her, she was overwhelmed. Attention was to her like water to a thirsty person. When Derrick began petting, wanting more, and pushing to "go all the way," Janet submitted because she wanted his love and attention more than anything else. Once he bedded her, he moved on to another girl and left Janet without so much as a good-bye. She reacted with a loss of appetite, refused to attend school, longed desperately for the relationship she thought she had lost, and eventually, was hospitalized for depression.

While Janet's reaction was extreme, variations of her pain are common. The aftermath of sex for a girl often carries with it humiliation. She realizes the male's attention was fundamentally motivated by lust not by her as a person. She waits for that call the next day to see what it meant to him. All too often the call does not come until he is in the mood for more sex. Meanwhile, he is likely to "kiss and tell" and her reputation is ruined.

Inexperienced males are often unsatisfying lovers due to their eagerness and selfishness. The male has an orgasm, the girl does not. She does not know what an orgasm is supposed to feel like. She is likely to experience pain and discomfort while the male reaches orgasm.

Many of our female clients report they hardly knew what was happening during their first intercourse but they do recall it was painful and degrading. While the male felt great they felt let down. Where was the romance? The bells? The loving talk? The commitment? With no friends to confide in, girls also have to deal with the aftermath of sex in isolation. Confusion becomes spiced with guilt.

Females have a different mind set about sexuality than men, partly because the consequences are so different for them. There is the palpable fear of pregnancy. The negative effects for females who become pregnant includes life long responsibility for a child, the fear, horror and shame of an abortion, or the heartache of a miscarriage. Even the diseases they may acquire are more damaging to their bodies and minds than they are for males.

Different Dreams And Fantasies

The two sexes have different orientations to the future as we can see by their life dreams. Beginning with play fantasy, girls develop an idea of their future which includes finding the perfect man, making the perfect marriage, having wonderful children, being an ideal wife to a perfect husband, and living in a dream home.

Boys have dreams of doing things, having adventures and conquests. As they mature, they focus on career. They're not concerned about whom they'll meet but with what they'll do in the world. Family will become a part of their lives, not a preoccupation.

In adolescence, girls begin their search for a partner who will fulfill their dream of security, love, marriage and family. When men and women do get married, women see themselves as achieving their goals. Men are ambivalent about the marriage because they take on so much responsibility and give up so much of their mandated autonomy.

They have to give up adventure and sexual athleticism for the restrictive routine of marriage. Consider the quite different ways that women and men approach marriage through the practice of showers and bachelor parties.

The *shower* is a happy occasion in which the bride-to-be is attended by female relatives and friends who bring her gifts to prepare her for domestic life. She is admired, encouraged and congratulated. Showers are a celebration of the change in her status from single to married, from being without a man to having one, from being taken care of by her family or herself to being taken care of by a husband.

The *bachelor party* for the husband-to-be teases him because he must now leave the life of the casual male to assume obligations and lose his freedom. His pre-marriage party includes a last drunken binge, "stag" movies, and all manner of reminders that he's "biting the dust" as an independent, autonomous person. He's bid farewell from the good life of the carefree male.

If there's so much to lose by getting married, why do men do it? Here are three possible explanations:

1. If a man doesn't propose marriage on a timely schedule, the woman lets him know she won't wait forever. The pressure is on; she wants to progress to a legitimate relationship—if not with him, then with someone else. He must commit or lose her.

2. Men seek a sexual partner who will be constantly available and readily accessible.

3. Males tire of the dating scene and trade this for the satisfaction of domestic life while they follow their career interests. The expectation for men is that they will marry when they can support a family.

Naturally, both women and men learn to compromise their dreams with reality. This is often a painful process because they have such different expectations in life they can as easily grow apart as together.

How Women and Men Confuse Love and Sex

The authors strongly believe that while men and women are basically similar as human beings, their differences are magnified in close relationships. This is evident in sexual relationships. A problem originates in the different emphasis and value women and men place on love and sex.

They both make distinctions between sex and love but they do it in distinct ways. Men can separate sex from love whereas women see sex as a component of love. Men express their love through sex; women must love and be loved before they are most comfortable with sex.

If a woman discovers that her man has been having extramarital sex, she loses trust in him. Women are typically baffled and enraged by men who protest that extramarital sex is "just sex, nothing serious," and that it should not destroy the relationship. Men make their apologies, then want the relationship to continue as before. They do not want to dwell on the past. The man's view is, "I did it, I'm sorry, I'll never do it again. And now let's forget about it." Women cannot fathom how men say, mean, and believe that sex can be considered separate from love and obligation.

Men may truly love their wives and children and have no intention of breaking up the family when they engage in extramarital sex. The fact that they have sex with someone other than their wife may not change their view of their family or their marital commitment.

Sex is sex; love is love. Men can experience one without the other. For example, they can have sex with prostitutes but not fall in love with them. If men typically loved the women they had sex with, they would either love many women or "commit" to the first one they had sex–love with. To confuse matters further, men also experience love-making as an expression of intimacy with the woman they love. It may be difficult for women to know whether they're being lusted or loved. Men aren't always sure which is which.

The way men separate love, sex, and commitment can be seen in the way they establish extramarital relationships with women they supposedly "love": The "other woman." Men can compartmentalize their lives which enables them to take a lover, promise her they will leave their wives (eventually) but never do it. They declare their love for both women: for the wife out of habit, commitment, and her virtues; to the lover for excitement and variety as well as a claim to their old freedoms. This leaves the "other woman" waiting patiently, painfully, and indefinitely for her "lover" to commit. If women understood men, they would be less prone to continue these painful relationships. They would understand men are quite capable of having sex, even a relationship, without being fully committed. Women would be in a better position if they could comprehend that sex, love, and commitment are separable in the male's mind.

Paradoxically, when a man loves a woman, or wants to express his love for her, he is prone to express it through sex. He seldom writes poetry to her. Another way he has of showing his love is to excel in his work so he can give her the things he thinks she wants.

If the object of his affection refuses to make love with him though she claims she loves him, he finds this incomprehensible. He cannot fathom love without sex. His way of expressing love is to *make* love.

How Women Separate Love and Sex

Do women separate love from sex and if so, under what circumstances and how?

Whereas men easily engage in sex without love or commitment, women are more interested in relationships *with* love; sex is but one aspect of the total package. Their strong inclination is to reserve sex for the person they love.

A survey by the Center for Disease Control (1989) found that of 962 Michigan women 80 percent had at least three sexual partners by the age of 35. Six percent of them had more than 25 partners. Men, as expected, have more sexual partners than do women. (This means either that relatively few women are having a lot of sex with the available men or that there are many more women than there are men.)

If women have casual sex, i.e., without love and commitment, they generally do not feel good about it. Sex is more agreeable to them if it is with a person they love. You are unlikely to hear a woman reminisce with a sense of pride and achievement about all the sexual partners she has had. In contrast, many men look back at their multiple sexual partners with an ego-enhancing sense of self-satisfaction. Unlike women, they are known to brag openly about their conquests.

Another problem arises when, after the relationship is established, a woman loves her man but does not feel as sexual toward him as he does toward her. The man feels unloved if his woman is less interested in sex than he is. When he hassles her for sex, she is disappointed that he cannot love her for herself, i.e., without sex. Whereas many women can love without needing sex, men see sex as a necessary ingredient of love.

Men separate and combine love and sex in unusual ways. They can have sex with women they do not love and still desire sex from the woman they do love—even demand it. This brings no end of confusion to women whose spouses have been unfaithful. Typically, these women search for answers in something they have done wrong, some shortcomings of their

own, or in some way the other woman
outclasses them. At lease in the initial stages of
discovering infidelity, no matter how angry and
hurt they are, women often assign themselves
some measure of self-blame.
"Why," she asks, "did he do this to me?"
Has she not given this man her best? Even if
she has not been amorous with her husband,
she has shown him love in other ways. She's
been a good mother and wife, done special
things for him. What the female does not
understand is that the male is quite capable of
loving one woman and having sex with her and
with others he does not love—simultaneously.

Paula and Sy have been married four years. During
two of those years they got along well and had a good
sex life despite the fact both had sexual inhibitions
stemming from their strict religious upbringing. Unable
to conceive a child, they entered a fertility program and
eventually had a child. Their lovemaking became so
medical and mechanical, and the pregnancy meant so
much to them, they abstained from sex during the
pregnancy to avoid guilt if she aborted.

Paula was tired after Patrick's birth and found it
difficult to participate in sex. Sy became dissatisfied and
withdrawn and found a series of "girlfriends" that
pumped up his ego and satisfied his needs. He didn't
love them but he needed sex. It also provided him with
confirmation that he was a fully functioning male.

When Paula discovered one of his affairs, she was
crushed. She could not understand his explanation; he
felt she had encouraged him to find sex elsewhere. He
had no intention of leaving her and the baby but this
hardly consoled her.

He begged for her understanding. They did
eventually reconcile but they still have some of the same

problems relating to sex, love and commitment. However, Sy no longer cheats because he is too afraid of losing his family. Paula still doesn't trust him.

Paula and Sy's problems are far from over. Until they deal with their significantly different views of love and sex, they are likely to experience further disturbances in the relationship.

However, when a man discovers a wife's infidelity, he may conclude his wife does not love him. He's more likely to be correct! How could she love him if she slept with someone else? He's been trained to expect the greater loyalty of women to men.

How to Make Use Of Knowledge About Sexual Differences

What do these sexual differences between women and men mean to you? How can you use this information in your life?

1. **Realize and accept** the fact that, however meritorious your own ideas and feelings about sexual intimacy are, your partner has some just as dear to him/her. If you give indications that his/her preferences are unacceptable or abnormal, you block an important avenue of intimacy. All of us have been trained to be restrained and secretive about our sexual desires and practices. In an intimate relationship, the participants should discuss sexual issues with one

another; issues they would not reveal to others. If you read the advice columns, you'll find men and women asking for help in understanding what happened to sex after marriage. They ask advice columnists because they cannot discuss secret thoughts and feelings with their partners. A high priority in any intimate relationship should be open communication about the very subjects we were trained as children and adolescents to avoid.

2. **To improve your sexual relationship**, pleading, becoming angry, degrading the other, or withdrawing will **not** get you the results you want. We recommend that you discuss sexual issues from the standpoint that you are having feelings about what you need and are not getting. You can also indicate that what is happening to you is making it difficult for you to fully enjoy the relationship.

Use "I" not "you" statements. Say, "I feel like I'm not loved when I experience rejection." Don't say, "You make me feel rejected when you withhold sex from me." Most people are sensitive about their adequacy as lovers. Anything you say to diminish the other person's self-esteem will make it more difficult to solve the problem.

We referred earlier to Doug and Cindy who were at odds about how often they should have sex. Her inclinations were to have sex about twice a month. He thought every other day would be about right for him. She took his perception of frequency to mean she was sexually inadequate and sought to defend her self-esteem. He took her defense as a sign that she was not interested in change. Therefore, he lost his feelings for her.

Once they thoroughly aired their differences he had to make a difficult decision that took her lower sex drive into consideration. Doug would have to accommodate himself to less than he desired if he wanted to stay married. He ruled out divorce or extramarital affairs.

Cindy realized she was not entirely pleasing to him sexually. Once relieved of her guilt and defensiveness about sex, she felt freer to have him request sex as well as for her to say no. He made more requests for sex and she refused more often. However, the net result was that she said "yes" significantly more often than she had before they worked out their understanding.

3. **Get some outside help** before sexual difficulties become firmly entrenched. If you're the one to suggest therapy, indicate that you need help to change yourself to improve the relationship. Don't cast blame on him or he will defend himself and you'll both lose an important opportunity for change.

4. **If you do not seek counseling** to help air and correct sexual difficulties, find some other means to let the other person know how

you feel and what *you* think about the problem. If the other person does not know something is troubling you, how can that person adjust? The simplest method of bringing the problem up for consideration is to let the other person know tactfully but clearly how you feel and think. Remember to use "I" statements; do not attack or assign blame to the other person.

Despite having knowledge about sexual differences, there are male/female barriers to sexual intimacy that sometimes confound and confuse relationships. These differences are clarified in the following chapter, Barriers To Sexual Intimacy.

BARRIERS TO SEXUAL INTIMACY

> We identify love with emotional expression and talking about feelings, aspects of love that women prefer and in which women tend to be more skilled than men. ...We often ignore the instrumental and physical aspects of love that men prefer. This feminized perspective leads us to believe that women are much more capable of love than men and that the way to make relationships more loving is for men to become more like women.
> —*Francesca M. Cancian*

Carla, 27, married to Mark for three years, spoke with considerable pain and sadness: "In the beginning we talked a lot, we shared everything. We couldn't wait to get together to exchange thoughts and feelings. Talking to each other was our favorite thing to do. It was what convinced me Mark was the man for me. I had never been this close to a human being before.

"Then we married and things changed. He seemed to distance himself from me. When I brought it to his attention Mark simply said, 'I'm so busy trying to make headway on the job, securing our future, I just don't have time or energy to sit and talk like we used to.' Eventually, I could not deny I felt he was losing interest in me. It was hard to accept. I wanted him to be my best friend and my husband, but he slipped away."

Do you identify with Carla? Hasn't her husband disappointed and frustrated her by not loving her, intimately, *her* way? Love relationships often begin with the sharing of histories, philosophies of life, emotions, private experiences, values and secrets. Stir in sexual intimacy and the brew becomes a *powerful, blinding love potion.*
Unfortunately, our expectations are all too often dashed after the courtship. The original flush of intimacy and hot romance usually disappears as a relationship unfolds. At the very least, it changes. At best, romance becomes a deepening, equally gratifying loveship. How you deal with love and intimacy may determine your own fate.

Love: Men's Or Women's Definitions?

With the rise of feminism, women seem to have cornered the market on what a love relationship *really* is. Therefore, men's style of loving is regarded as deficient. Is it a victory for women that their version of love is accepted? Perhaps.
Instead of choosing sides as to which sex knows, *really* knows, how to love, it is preferable to understand that **women and men are different. Each sex has a valid approach to love.** To choose one way over the other is to increase the likelihood that no one will be satisfied.
There is a strong tendency for each sex to assume that his or her way is the right way.

Once a point of view is established, it is difficult to even reconsider it, let alone change it. However, if you *accept and respect the differences* between women and men and are not judgmental, you can begin to improve your relationship.

Expressive Versus Instrumental Love

Francesca M. Cancian (1986) from whose article we took the chapter's opening quotation, clarifies how women and men differ in their perspectives of love and intimacy. She spells out the consequences of the feminization of love.

Women have an *expressive* loving style that includes affection, emotion, tenderness, intimacy, self-expression, openness, passion, sharing of confidences, disclosure of one's inner life, warmth, talkativeness, and empathy.

Men have an *instrumental* loving style based on providing practical help, sharing physical activities, spending time together, providing security, being responsible for the partner's well-being, providing material things, and sex. According to Cancian, "...sexual intercourse seems to be the most meaningful way of giving and receiving love for many men" (p. 78). It is—whether it is "politically correct" or not—one of the ways men communicate their love.

To disrespect the natural way another person loves is to negate that person. It is better to understand and incorporate your differences.

Men Have Their Way Of Loving

The fact that men express their love through sex often angers and confuses women. Women learn that men are adept at having sex without love and they disapprove of it. Should men therefore be condemned because they are different? If you're judgmental, will it improve your relationship?

As true as it is that men can and do separate love and sex, it is also true sex can be the most meaningful way men receive and give love. To improve your relationships you have to understand and accept gender differences as real and legitimate. If you can't do this, you are in for a never ending struggle and ultimate frustration.

Consider this statement: "Only women are loving." If you believe this perhaps you also believe that men are genetically incapable of loving or they are socialized not to love. The truth is, men *are* loving. But, they are loving in their own way. This makes them *different*, not superior, inferior or deficient. Men must also recognize and respect how women love. Each gender has strengths to bring to a relationship.

Cancian further argues that a *feminized* perspective of love works against women and encourages their devaluation and exploitation. How so? The feminized definition of love holds that men are louts; they are seen as unemotional, distant, not needing love. Yet, women want and need what men have and can give to women: money, a home, security, status, power, and love.

This need for what men can give them makes women dependent upon men. The feminized notion of love holds that women need love more than men do. What do women have that men need? Sex! Feminists often accuse men of pursuing sex without love. In contrast, most women are fulfilled sexually only when they have sex with love. According to this feminist definition, it then follows that men are deficient lovers and cannot satisfy women's needs.

The "men as deficient lover" formula leads us into an escape proof trap. The escape from this no win approach is to act on the belief that the sexes are *different* and to *respect* these differences.

Differences In Loving

Women and men have different versions of love. If women insist the only kind of love that is valuable is *expressive,* and men give love in an *instrumental* way, women are courting frustration.

Sex can be a part of love or lust. Men often experience love through sex whereas women experience sex as a part of love. Women may therefore feel that men are *using* them for their own pleasure. They want a different kind of love, one that Cancian called "Feminized."

A feminized version of love requires both parties to be mutually vulnerable, admit their weaknesses, and accept help. This conception of love is in conflict with masculine notions of intimacy. Should men give up their style of intimacy, based on "doing things together and for one another, and adopt a style favored by women? Or, should women give up their notion of love and convert to the male expression of love and intimacy? More to the point, is it possible to give up that which is natural to you and equally enjoy something that is not? Our position is that women and men have to bridge this gap between them, not insist that their way is the only way.

We can better explore the differences between the sexes if we clarify what *intimacy* means.

Intimacy

We may desire intimacy or avoid it but often we don't have a clear understanding of what *it* is. If we are confused about intimacy, it will be more difficult if not impossible to achieve.

According to Erik Erikson (1950) *intimacy* involves both a relationship commitment, and the sharing of one's inner-self in detail and depth. Men seem to have less inclination to be intimate and may have less access to their inner lives than women. Therefore, it is more difficult to get close to a man, especially at the emotional level. Men can be physically close to women when sex is involved but they generally have problems recognizing and disclosing their feelings.

Self-Defeating Love

Cancian points out how self-defeating the feminization of love is. If a woman seeks intimacy her way—shared vulnerability, tenderness, and self-disclosure—she ends up becoming more dependent upon the man because he then has what she wants yet is unlikely to be able to deliver it.

He in turn perceives (at some level) that she is making up the rules for love and he is not going to be able to live up to them. He withdraws. To the woman this may seem like withholding. "You've got it, why won't you give it to me? Are you punishing me? Don't you love me?"

As she intensifies her efforts to promote intimacy, he resolutely resists it, partly because he doesn't know what she wants. This promotes the very cycle of conflict that women wish to avoid. Neither party is happy, neither of them is fulfilled. The relationship suffers and it is the relationship she depends upon for her inner most sense of well-being.

A Better Way To Love

Cancian prefers an orientation to love which accepts both masculine and feminine qualities of love as "...necessary parts of a good love relationship" (p. 171). An excessively feminized perspective of love separates the sexes rather than harmonizes them.

If men and women express love differently, they can't expect to have it only their own way. If women want to close the gap between themselves and men, it is counter productive to reject men's ways of loving. How can we increase intimacy between the sexes? One method is through *closeness*.

Psychological Closeness

Psychological closeness refers to the frequency and depth of self-disclosure, the willingness to share with another person one's innermost thoughts about self. Frequency of sharing is important in an intimate relationship.

The depth of self-disclosure is critical since sharing one's inner thoughts and feelings increases bonding. Intimacy develops when one trusts enough to reveal the inner-self and has faith the other person will not use these revelations to intimidate or inflict pain later.

This last point merits emphasis: If you wish to encourage sharing of self, *under no circumstances should you ever use the information that you acquire to embarrass, humiliate or shame the other person*. If you do this once, you significantly decrease the likelihood that you will be trusted again. Bill and Melanie's relationship suffered from the problems they had in establishing closeness.

Melanie, a physical therapist, has a beautiful, slim face and an unusually elongated, fragile appearance; Bill, a fireman, resembles a suma wrestler.

Melanie and Bill lived together for a year and learned not to trust one another. When Melanie, 36, and Bill, 40, finally sought therapy, Melanie complained about the futility of her efforts to get Bill to discuss or make commitments about their future. In fact, Bill seldom confided in Melanie about anything.

In a misguided effort to force Bill to be closer to her, Melanie demanded that he leave the apartment and he did. Later, she changed her mind and wanted him to move back. To her consternation, he refused to return.

Melanie said, "I thought he'd miss me so much he would want to marry me so he wouldn't lose me. Instead, he says that he wants to be with me but he's never here. When I want to talk about it, he says things like, 'Are you through?' "

Bill saw the situation differently: "We talked it over, up and around until there wasn't anything more to say on the subject. But, Still it never gets settled. She always brings up something I said or did in the past; there's no end to it. So, why even get into it? It's ridiculous. I agreed to counseling on the slim chance you could help us settle something—anything. We're deadlocked. I'm not interested in going over and over the same issues or hearing about something I said or did in the past. If these counseling sessions end up as nothing but a rehash of the past, I won't be ...."

Before Bill could finish, Melanie interrupted, "I can't help bringing up things he's said in the past. When I remember something, I feel as if I *have* to say it because I want to settle the issue. I either want to get married or end the relationship. But, he won't say 'yes' he'll marry me or 'no' he won't." Bill said it wasn't that simple. He feared if he spoke his mind, Melanie would take his words out of context and use them against him.

Even if Melanie's complaints are justified, they are presented counter-productively. When words become a sword instead of a bridge between people, intimacy is the casualty. For Bill and Melanie, letting go of the past and living in the present became a first order therapy issue.

Some therapists refer to the tactic of using stored-up anger to win arguments as "kitchen sinking": Everything but the kitchen sink is thrown into the fray. To create a safe relationship environment requires that the problem under consideration be discussed for what it is, not for what it *has been*. There's a tendency to use things from the past to "win" the present argument. However, we *strongly recommend against this tactic*.

As Melanie redoubled her efforts to help Bill understand her position, she saw and felt Bill retreat. Nevertheless, she felt compelled to emphasize how "wrong" his position was. Eventually, the therapy took effect. There was an amazing turnaround in their relationship when Melanie grasped the idea that she was working against her self-interests.

A key factor in Melanie's ability to improve her understanding of Bill, herself, and the situation was her realization that men in general—and Bill in particular—have a different approach to intimacy and communication. Melanie's need to turn Bill into the intimate person she thought she wanted was replaced by an effort to appreciate who he was and how he communicated warmth and closeness. She really understood and integrated his personhood into her feelings. He, in turn, could now listen to what she said and tried to understand it. He wanted to give her what she wanted when he could.

They both reached an understanding that women and men are different: 1. Each gender develops an intimacy style during socialization; 2. Neither the man's style nor the woman's is the "right" way.

Thereafter, Melanie reported feeling happier with herself than she had for years and Bill began to feel comfortable and safe. She was able to consider what he was saying from his point of view and share her thoughts with him without trying to *persuade* him. Once convinced that what he said was given equal weight and would not be thrown up to him later, Bill's sharing increased. He never got as good at it as Melanie but this new style allowed the couple to be intimate, each in their own way.

Mutual Sharing

Mutual sharing promotes closeness. If only one person does the sharing, the relationship is unbalanced. One shares many intimate details of their life with a therapist. Yet, few clients or therapists claim they are *close* to one another. This is because therapists are professionally limited in what they may reveal about themselves. Clients are often curious about the therapist at a personal level but must adjust themselves to the inequality in self-disclosure. The absence of equitable sharing limits the range of a relationship.

The freedom to talk about anything that comes to mind, negative or positive, is one dimension of intimacy. The most intimate relationships, then, are those in which the parties disclose things about themselves they ordinarily would keep secret. They suspend their fears of being judged negatively or of losing self-esteem.

A few cautions about self-disclosure are necessary. Sharing secrets requires good judgment. There are parts of almost everyone's life that are best kept to one's self. For instance, you might be asked about your sexual history. Suppose you talk about two previous sexual relationships and the new person in your life wants to know the details. He urges, "Describe your sexual relationship. Where did you do it? How? Who did what? How does sex with them compare to sex with me?" Approach such requests with utmost care. You may reveal things you wish you hadn't, and there's no turning back.

A second warning about disclosure is that once something is shared it should *never* be used to attack or berate the other person in any way. When personal information is used against an individual she/he becomes cautious or refuses to disclose any more.

Intimacy Is Different For The Two Sexes

Since we tend to put a high premium on intimacy, we may not realize people also require distance and privacy in an intimate relationship. When one person wants more distance or intimacy than the other, stress and dissatisfaction are heightened. The solution?

Accept the other person's needs for closeness and distance as valid, for them. Then begin to work your way, by mutual consent, toward a level of intimacy that does not violate the other person's needs. If you insist on intimacy that suits you, the other person will take counter measures to secure himself against your intrusions. Distance, not closeness, will be the result. This happened with Kathy and Josh.

> Kathy, 37, came to therapy because of a problem her husband was having and hastened to tell us the difficulty was not a "marital problem." She described her relationship with Josh, 37, as excellent, especially since they each brought children from previous marriages into the household. Everyone was adjusting well.
>
> Kathy looked disheveled. Her hair was unkempt with combs stuck in to corral stray curls, her shirt was partially ironed, and her speech was tentative—as though her thoughts were in error.
>
> The few "minor" issues that troubled her included her husband's job loss, his absence from home for long hours and his drinking. Her dilemma? She did not want to hurt his feelings by calling these things to his attention. She reported that each of them scrupulously avoided saying things that damaged the other's self-image.
>
> We gave this couple high marks on self-restraint but low marks on intimacy. When Josh came to see us, he was openly offended by our reference to his marital difficulty. He insisted there was no marital problem. Instead, he wanted us to understand he was highly anxious and needed help to relax. But, he didn't want to talk about it. Josh wanted a quick fix without revealing his inner thoughts and feelings.

This husband and wife unintentionally conspired to reduce their conflict by avoiding its source. They were trying to maintain their distance but this only increased the problems between them. The distance they established left them so remote they could not share enough to improve the relationship. In fact, when they realized they would have to share more of themselves in therapy than they shared at home, they terminated.

Intimacy Hurdles

Given all the impediments to closeness and intimacy between the sexes we must marvel at how well people actually adapt to one other. Perhaps people try so hard to get close to one another because they have been socialized in groups and cannot renounce human companionship. On the other hand, group interference in individual lives is a universal problem. Why is establishing the right degree of intimacy such a problem?

Several forces create barriers to intimacy between men and women—more so than between members of the same sex.

Socialization

Gender roles are in place before we are born. They are transmitted to us in subtle ways, become integral parts of our personalities and remain largely unquestioned. Even when we find feminine and masculine roles stultifying we have difficulty changing them. Saudi women defiantly drove automobiles in Riyadh in 1990. They were arrested, and the rules—supposedly religious in origin—against females driving were enforced. (The Saudis will be hard pressed to keep women out of the driver's seat forever.)

Social pressures to conformity aside, we usually can't get outside our own conditioning to view a problem objectively. If we rebel against cultural definitions, we are in for a battle. Many forces are aligned against us.

As adults we have the same needs we did as teenagers: To march to our peers' cadence. Most people are not mavericks so they conform—most of the time and in most ways—to social rules. Society and culture define the proper levels of intimacy and these are different for each sex. There are explanations as to why and how this happens.

All societies define men's and women's roles differently. Women rear the children and men are the warriors—there are few exceptions to this arrangement. In all societies, men are the keepers of the weapons. It is not difficult to see why men are the warriors; they have strength and size advantages.

Theoretically, women could bear the children, then turn them over to the men to raise. But, this does not occur in any known society. What does happen is that all children are expected to be either female or male in attitude and behavior.

There are different ideas and variations about how children are gendered and socialized into their sex roles. Psychoanalysts have charted the different paths girls and boys take in growing up. This is important to recognize if you want to understand gender differences. What follows is an elaboration of an idea introduced in the last chapter.

Boys Must Give Up Mother To Become Men

All children begin with an attachment to the primary care giver. This is usually the mother. The critical issue is that the boy must surrender his primary identification with the mother—therefore, with all women—so he can become a man. He must identify with the father and men, thereby creating a gap between himself and females.

Girls do not have to make this change. They remain identified with the mother and the feminine way of loving. Girls stay close, almost fused, with mother. They don't undergo the separations from mother boys do. This has significant consequences later in life.

We are familiar with the occasional boy too attached to his mother. He is derisively referred to as a "mama's boy." When a similar observation is made about a girl, she's merely "close to her mother"; no pathology is implied.

Problems arise when males and females form relationships in later life. Having been separated for so long, by adolescence girls and boys are a mystery to one another. They don't know how to behave with one another and they spend much of their energy trying to figure out what the other sex is all about.

In summary, a woman has learned to be close to her mother and has a built-in notion of what intimacy is; intimacy is the closeness she has with mom. A boy has to learn to be masculine. But, for this he pays the price of having to distance himself from mother (women). He learns the masculine way of relating to others, thereby insuring that he will not be understood by women. Though both sexes want closeness and intimacy, they have different perspectives of what these are.

The Emotional Wall

The invisible barrier between the sexes can be characterized as an *emotional wall.* The wall isn't as prominent during courtship since males are romantic and tend to equate sex and their desire for sex with closeness. He pays a great deal of attention to the woman initially and she often mistakes his focus for closeness. Romance and courtship seem to breach the emotional wall. We say "seems to" because once the couple is married and the romance fades, they have a clearer view of how different they are.

Donna (Chapter Three) referred to her sexuality during the courtship as an "altered state," one in which she seemed to melt into the personality of her lover. While the female bonds by becoming a part of the male, the male's boundaries generally stay intact. He may be in an altered state but it has less to do with the experience of intimacy than with the excitement of romance and sexuality. In short, after the flush of romance, each person returns to their natural state. The woman seeks the same feeling of closeness she had with her mother. She may have wanted a similar blending with her father, or she may have had a close relationship with her father and wishes to re–establish herself as an object of adoration with her husband. Once the honeymoon is over, the husband is likely to re-establish his familiar distance from the woman. Ted's life illustrates this point.

Ted, a 41 year-old professional musician, attended his parents' forty-fifth anniversary. An aunt he had not seen for many years was at the party. This reawakened powerful feelings he hadn't experienced since childhood. When he was seven, his brother contracted a terminal disease. He was sent to his aunt's while the family saw to the brother's illness and grieved his death.

Ted's mother was a competent but emotionally distant woman. His father, a passive man, allowed his wife to run the family and him. When Ted was sent to his aunt, he was ill-prepared for the warmth of her home. He vividly remembers Aunt Sue playing games with him, taking an interest in him, and gladly seeing to his needs.

The reunion awakened sweet memories and Ted wanted to talk with his Aunt about the powerful childhood experiences she had unknowingly provided and to express his gratitude for her kindness. However, he could not bring himself to speak. Consciously, he feared others in the family would find out.

Find out what? That he was sentimental? He feared he'd lose his protective armor.

What about his own marriage?
Ted's wife, Lola, 40, had difficulty understanding
why he was so elusive when she did everything she
could to promote a close caring relationship between
them. She persisted in her quest for intimacy although
when she was pregnant with the first of their four
children he had threatened to divorce her.

We explored his divorce threat. One part of
his fantasy was that he feared being replaced in
Lola's affections by a baby, especially a
daughter. His mother had been closer to her
own daughters than to her sons. Ted's
conditioning appeared to set up a no win
situation that insured marital unhappiness. He
needed closeness but felt rejected by his own
mother. His early developmental
disappointments became a blueprint used to
relate to all women. He wanted to get closer
but could not get past the emotional wall built
during his childhood.

Breaking Down Intimacy Barriers

What can be done in a situation like this?
How do we take down these emotional walls?
Is it possible? Irving and Suzanne Sarnoff
(1989) argue that the past does not represent
a barrier to intimacy:

> Contrary to prevailing stereotypes, ...the quality of a
> couple's marriage is not defined by similarities or
> differences in their individual backgrounds and
> personalities. Rather, marriage is a shared conception of
> how mates agree to love one another and to express their

fear of loving. Spouses jointly and equally create these agreements in the here-and-now of their direct interactions, and they can always decide to make rational changes for their common good (p. 55).

The Sarnoff's view is a hopeful one since it allows for change; couples determine their own fate, it isn't determined for them. The Sarnoffs believe that spouses create marital arrangements on the basis of current conceptions. They are free to make any arrangements they want to.

You now have two distinct views about intimacy and distance. One says any barriers can be removed with some ease and the other suggests the foundations of these walls run very deep and are hard to penetrate.

However, we want to point out one phrase in the Sarnoff quote, "...to express their fear of loving." The Sarnoffs do not tell us where this fear of loving comes from but we will provide you with our ideas about their origins.

We agree with the perspective that once children are programmed these patterns influence the rest of their lives. We also agree with the Sarnoffs; change is possible. Still, we believe such changes are made with great difficulty. It has not been our experience that people easily "choose" how they shall love one another or choose to rid themselves of deeply ingrained patterns or fears about intimacy.

If change from a distant to an intimate style of loving between the sexes is to happen, it will probably begin in courtship.

Courtship, Sex, and Emotional Needs

When a couple falls in love the outside world dims leaving the couple in their own fantasy, focused on one another. They are interested in every aspect of the other, continually touching, saying loving things to one another and spending many intimate hours together. Each lover has feelings like none they've ever had before. As they undergo this emotional bonding, the other is perceived as perfect, extraordinary, and wonderful. The *ego ideal* has been found and engaged in love. Both parties are exhilarated. Self-esteem is elevated and their world is filled with pleasures. The sun always shines. They can't do without one another. This is Everywoman's dream of how she will fall in love with that special man.

During courtship the female is more open to sex and may even be eager for sex. She is also likelier to put his needs first, second and third because she wishes to please him. She is sexually stimulated by her love and her desire to bond. She wants to be a good lover, giving him pleasure. His pleasure is her pleasure.

As part of the courtship, the male intuitively knows or is told by the female that she expects feelings between them to deepen. He displays his love through his interest and attention to her. He takes action. He takes her places, buys her flowers, wants to be with her. He is unlikely to express his feelings as often as she does, but his emotional output is heightened throughout the courtship. They talk for long hours together. They are perfectly suited to one another. He's never opened up to anyone like this before. Will it last?

Because women are programmed to take care of the male and the relationship, women work hard to create an atmosphere in which the male can show his vulnerable, emotional side. Mutual emotionality is likelier to occur during the heat of the courtship than to flower after the marriage.

Slowly, as the couple emerges from romantic bliss into the real world—usually after marriage—the love cocoon becomes porous. Extraordinary love making becomes ordinary and unlikely to reach those ecstatic courtship heights again. As the relationship matures women find themselves less interested in sexual intercourse. The male's sex drive is likelier to persist.

For men, being sexually active is being alive and satisfied. It elevates self-esteem and confirms their manhood. Sex is likely to have an imperative quality, like a thirst that must be quenched. For women, being touched, caressed, kissed and hugged is the source of major satisfaction. Sex can become bothersome (unless he shows a sudden disinterest).

The difference between male and female loving is more evident when there is conflict, anger or other negative emotions. It then becomes difficult for a woman to be relaxed and sexual. She needs to settle the difficulty before she is interested in sex. Men, on the other hand, often want to "make up" and put things right by making love. There is, in the male ethos, a notion that the cure for whatever ails a woman is a "good f___."

Men are extraordinarily poor at reading what's on a woman's mind and what she wants. A man is likely to think the female is punishing him by refusing sex. This may be true. It may also be true that for the moment she finds the relationship in such disrepair she is sexually turned off.

Occasionally when relationships are crumbling, what is left of the emotional bond may be expressed through sex. In Stephanie's case, she felt that sex was the last thin strand holding the relationship together.

Stephanie carefully eased into the office as though she wanted to hide. She was so tightly wound that her emotionally charged delivery nearly overwhelmed me. A tear appeared now and then as she described her life. She was a failure, she said. She had done everything, *everything*, to make her husband happy.

"We are sexually compatible. In fact, our sex life is wonderful," Stephanie reported. She regards herself as a thirty-six-year-old failure because, after turning herself inside out for her husband, 37, he left the home and rented an apartment.

Stephanie, a housewife, could not understand how her life had deteriorated so completely when she had worked so hard at the relationship. From the moment they met in high school Stephanie looked up to John as a smarter person with more poise than herself. He was from a family that had "more class" than her own. When John occasionally dated other girls, Stephanie was heartbroken. She thought his dating was a result of her inadequacies, her inability to make him happy.

He was secretive about his activities with other girls but somehow Stephanie always found out. She blamed herself. It did not occur to her that he acted out of his own self-interests and his desire for variety. He did not want to be her captive. Nevertheless, she got her man; in his junior year of college they were engaged and married.

Soon after John graduated and got his first job Stephanie became pregnant. John, arguing they could not afford a child, was so displeased, and objected so loudly Stephanie agreed to an abortion. She had miscalculated; she thought he was ready.

In later years she was disgusted and angry with herself for having the abortion. At the time, she agreed with John that they should be in a stable financial situation to have children. Two years later she decided to have a child and arranged to become pregnant. John was not thrilled to learn that he would be a father. He showed little interest when John Jr. was born.

Stephanie described herself as twirling around John, always focusing, without success, on what would make him happy. In turn, John criticized Stephanie. He told her not to talk and laugh so loudly, to be a better housekeeper, to wear her hair differently, and dress better.

Instead of defending herself, Stephanie redoubled her efforts to please him. Every day she scurried around in her mind, like a rat in a maze, desperately examining the corners of her mind for "the answer." She said, "I could hear myself babbling, trying to get his attention while knowing I was pushing him away with dull talk." He responded by withholding his approval, criticizing her more and spending less time at home.

During their sixteen years together, John's sexual interest in Stephanie became her love barometer. When his interest flagged, Stephanie became flirtatious to the point of sexual aggression. If they had sex and John seemed to enjoy it, Stephanie was ecstatic. This meant John loved her.

If John had to be coaxed and coerced to have sex, Stephanie could not sleep afterward because she saw this as a sign of his distance and her failure. To her, their sexual activity was the only semblance of closeness left in the marriage.

In the year prior to his leaving, John was seldom available sexually. When everything she tried failed, including making herself as alluring as possible, Stephanie turned her anger and frustration inward and sank into a depression. She summed up her life. "I am worn out, I feel ugly, I have no confidence, I haven't developed friendships, I'm socially inept, and worst of all I feel guilty as a mother because I've been so preoccupied trying to please John."

Responsibility for her children got Stephanie out of bed in the morning. But, the loss of her husband was disorienting. She felt lost, cried on and off all day, and continually ruminated about the past trying to understand where she had gone wrong. In this state of mind it was difficult to leave the house.

How could she have fallen so low? What brought her to this point?

In therapy, Stephanie learned that her personal history played an important role in her present difficulties. Her father had two jobs and was physically and emotionally distant. Her mother worked afternoons and was not emotionally available to her even when she was in the house.

As a little girl Stephanie felt left out and lonely. She resorted to pleasing people to get attention and carried this into her marriage. Stephanie always felt needy, always groveled for attention and grasped for love.

John was uncomfortable with Stephanie's efforts to please him. Although John enjoyed the attention, at the same time, he was uncomfortable and in a private session described his wife as, "Overbearing, too nice, too affectionate, too much for me." He said his critical attitude derived from his parents' household where people had to monitor behavior due to his mother's fear of what others might think.

Developing intimate relationships, feeling loved and close to others is imperative to women. As the little bit of remaining intimacy slipped through her grasp, Stephanie felt the substance of her life evaporating. The failure of others to respond and the elusiveness of the love she sought slowly depleted her confidence. Defeated in the struggle to please her husband, Stephanie's frail self-esteem withered.

Stephanie eventually worked through her difficulties. She cautiously but deliberately re-engaged with her mother, an aunt who had been a mother surrogate, and her sister. With the objective eye of the therapist exploring life with her, Stephanie saw and began to feel things differently. Eventually, she found she could depend on her family for support and discovered she was valued.

Stephanie's major progress was owed to a growing ability to identify what she wanted for herself as a person and what she wanted from others. She began working in her own best interest, ridding herself of her sensitivity to John's criticisms. Stephanie began building self-esteem by viewing herself differently, accepting and liking her looks, body and personality. She established friendships of her own and attended college. Eventually, she said, "I can feel a person emerging."

For Stephanie, touching was soothing; she felt connected and calm. For men, however, touching is not necessarily an intimate or pleasant experience. Instead, physical contact without a violent or clearly sexual in intent can be very threatening to men.

It is a form of *gender conceit* for either sex to assume that what is natural and comfortable for them is correct for everyone.

Differences In Touching

The simple act of touching another person has different meanings for women and men. Women are reassured and comforted by gentle touching. Men *affectionately* punch each other, slap backs and butts and regard a vigorous, rough—even physically damaging—contest as a good time. The contact has to be rough to avoid the implication that the touching has sexual undertones.

One of our clients, Pat, made a real effort to restore her affection for her husband. They could never talk about sex but when she joined a support group the leader encouraged her to tell her husband what she liked and disliked sexually. Pat shared this information at great risk because her husband was prone to take her comments about sex as an insult and a put-down. When she told him how she wanted to be touched *and* *w*here, he did so for a while but soon reverted to what *he* thought turned her on. That included rough touching and "dirty talking." His failure to take her sexual suggestions seriously helped her clarify his constant focus on himself; his thoughts and feelings predominated. Pat realized if she lived her life out with this man, she would dance to his tune; he was unable to view her as an individual or respect her desires.

How important is touching? It may even be important for health. In a study of male and female surgery patients touched by a nurse as she explained the surgical and post-surgical procedures, men regarded the experience as upsetting. Both their blood pressure and anxiety level rose and stayed elevated whereas women had a positive reaction. Touch lowered women's blood pressure and anxiety both before surgery and for more than an hour afterward.

It may be that touch threatens men because it reminds them of their dependency and vulnerability. Unless men initiate physical contact, it represents a lowering of power. People with higher status initiate touching. Few employees reach out and put their arms on their bosses' shoulders just as few women take the risk of initiating physical contact with a man with whom they are not intending to be intimate.

Body Attitudes and Intimacy

Since physical and emotional intimacy are closely related, the human body *should be* a primary source of satisfaction. Unfortunately, females often regard their bodies with distaste and seek to change their appearances in ways that are beyond their control. They perceive themselves as too fat, too thin, bulging or not bulging in the right places. Few women feel their bodies are just right. According to a 1990 survey of plastic surgeons, eighty-seven percent of all cosmetic surgeries were performed on women (*Longevity*, Sept. 1991).

Women carry a special burden when it comes to their bodies because they expect their figure to conform to the those hyped by the mass media. They want to feel good about themselves and they want to attract men.

These two major standard setters, the media and men, are often at odds since "slim is in" might be at loggerheads with the busty figure that men prefer. Research shows that men are *not* excessively concerned with bust size and shape. Women are! They are willing, if not eager, to undergo breast enhancing or reduction surgery even when the inserts (silicone) are potentially dangerous to their health.

Unforgiving standards for women's appearance creates a potent brew for self-discontent. The motivation for women seems to be that they conform to the "vogue," that which is being hyped at the moment. The "in" look is usually at odds with the natural female shape. These unrealistic expectations for the female body are probably at the root of the growing number of eating disorders.

Women who do not fit the popular body criteria or who "lose" their figures worry they will or will not be chosen by a man or be able to retain one on the basis of how they look. Women also "play to" other women. "False body consciousness" creates significant damage to women's self-esteem.

Since men are more powerful economically, they can attract younger women, more attractive women. What do younger women get from being with an older out-of-shape man? Their reward is social status, financial security and the multiple social advantages of basking in the achievements of the successful male. Another, but unlikely explanation is that young women are somehow strangely physically attracted to aging, potbellied, overweight and balding men. Or, perhaps young women by the millions seek older men because they have a father complex? Note: younger, prettier women are more attracted to "high status" older men.

When a woman feels self-conscious and negative about her body, it interferes with her sexuality and intimacy. She is likely to focus on what is wrong with her and how others view her. Under these circumstances, her self-esteem and self-confidence erode. This self-consciousness makes it more difficult for her to relate to others.

Studies of women's body image show that about 70 percent of women of all ages are significantly dissatisfied with some aspect of their appearance. Men are less concerned and less negative about their own appearance.

Since much of a woman's destiny, her treatment by others and her view of herself, is involved with her appearance, she devotes a great deal of money, worry, and action to looking "right." She must have the *right* clothes, the *right* breast size, the *right* weight, the *right* height, the *right* leg shape, the *right* thighs, the *right* hips, the *right* hair, even the *right* plastic surgeon. Whole industries promote and feed on women's fears about their bodies and appearance. "Snake oil" businesses profit in the billions from women's efforts to look young and look right.

Unfortunately, women constantly worry about their appearance, especially as they age. One of the first things a woman wants to know about a cheating husband is the age and looks of the other woman. She knows the rules of the competition: the younger, better shaped, sexier, and prettier woman gets the prize.

To Look Natural, Be Artificial

The distorted focus on correct appearance for females creates difficulties for both males and females. To men, women's efforts to be attractive seem like a deception. They complain about how much time and money women spend on their looks. However, a woman without make-up, a proper hair style and stylish clothes will not be well received by men or other women.

With this extreme concentration on appearance it is no wonder women are concerned about how they look when it is time to undress. Women often avoid disrobing in front of other women and some will go to any length not to be seen nude, especially by their husbands. Gail suffered terribly from body-image dissatisfaction:

> Gail, a twenty-nine-year-old secretary, sought therapy because she felt "squeezed" and overwhelmed with responsibility all the time.
> Gail said, "There isn't anything that is a pleasure in my life, including sex. It's so funny. When I met my husband, I was crazed. I actually desired sex, couldn't wait until we were together making love. I used to feel like I was panting just to be near him. Slowly that changed. Now I have no fire, no desire for him. Actually, I have no desire or time for sex, period. My

husband used to be in my dreams and daydreams, always in the front of my mind. Now he's in the back—if he's there at all. My whole life is bland. I'm anxious about what task has to be done next, where I have to go, what I have to do. Yet there is no way everything will get done."

Gail was glaringly obese but she avoided speaking about her weight for several months. One day she cautiously began with an admission, "My weight has always been a problem. When I was eleven I started gaining and I've been overweight ever since. When I met Dan I started losing weight and continued to lose until after the wedding. Since then, it's all been downhill and more pounds for me. Ever since I can remember, I've felt self-conscious about even the thought of being naked. Now it's ridiculous. I skulk around and go to any lengths not to let him see my body.

"I don't have any interest in sex. I'm not sure what is happening, whether it's my body or my endless duties or something physically wrong with me."

As therapy progressed, Gail revealed more about her husband's dissatisfaction with her appearance and her own obsession about weight. "Dan is a thirty-one-year-old physical fitness nut. He tells me he is turned off by my body. He doesn't want to go anywhere with me and if we go out to eat, he stares at me with what seems like anger if I eat a roll or order dessert. I'm caught! I can't lose weight; I've tried every diet. Every day I despise myself." Shortly after meeting Dan, when she was at her thinnest, Gail said, "It was just for a moment I accepted myself."

No longer able to accept herself, daily living became a burden. Her self-consciousness and ever present focus on body and weight left her in despair. She saw no way out of her difficulties. Her fat cells formed a solid wall between herself and her husband and any chance of full intimacy. His unhappiness with her appearance increased the distance between them.

Gail was adept at presenting herself as upbeat and carefree. She had been too ashamed to talk to anyone about her real self-feelings. In therapy she gradually freed herself from self-loathing. Gail began a weight loss program and is now in the process of slimming down. To her credit, she realizes she can be slimmer but never svelte. Her goals are realistic. It was not realistic to expect her to accept herself when all of those around her define her as unattractive.

Media Hype And Body Shame

Beauty, if not granted by nature, can be bought—so says the beauty industry. One of the richest self-made women in the world built her fortune on beauty products.

It will come as no surprise that 90% of advertisements in women's magazines are for beauty products and fashions. These magazines contain articles intended to beautify the body, improve and understand the mind, and to make women attractive socially and psychologically to men as well as to improve their self-acceptance.

The beauty industry is so successful that men are increasingly buying beauty products for themselves and are also looking for the right plastic surgeon. California, as usual, is in the vanguard of the latest fashion in surgery for males: Penis Enhancement. Fat cells are taken from elsewhere in the body and injected under the skin of the penis to increase its girth. (Some men have the surgery so they'll have a *bulge* in their pants; apparently this is a confidence booster.)

Men too make a contribution to women's discomfort with their appearance. Market researchers have found that the only common denominator for men of all classes is their dream of access to the culture's most attractive women and their fear of being rejected. From the marketers' perspective, the greater a man's anxiety about being rejected by women the likelier he is to buy the product promising he will gain the love of a beautiful woman.

Marketers tell us that young women dream about romance, a man, intimate relationships, security, and love. Television panders to women's dreams of romance and men's quest for sex. Most of the 785 million Americans who watch the Superbowl are men.

Ads for the Superbowl show beautiful, sexy women purring and looking adoringly either at one of the players or at a masculine, in-control male—while the product is displayed.

The message intended for the male viewer? These are the products a successful man should have if he is to get his woman (Warren Farrell, 1986). For the woman, these adverstisement are subliminal instructions for how they should behave and look to attract desirable men.

Body Watching

Men openly stare at women. They focus on the female body and are openly absorbed in contemplation and admiration of it. Men are encouraged to look at women and their figures. Women are also attentive to how men look, but learn to be subtle in their viewing.

The best-selling women's magazines (*Better Homes and Gardens* and *Family Circle*) focus on family, security, home beautification, cooking, and intimate relationships. Other popular magazines such as *Working Woman* are business oriented but the message of most of the articles focus on how to improve interpersonal situations.

In contrast, the best selling men's magazines—*Playboy, Sports Illustrated, Penthouse,* and *Forbes*—focus on sports, material possessions, politics and voyeuristic sex.

Pornography is thought to be incompatible with intimacy. In men's pornographic materials the theme is easy, anonymous, impersonal, unencumbered sex with an endless succession of hot, willing women. Women feel demeaned by the very thing that turn men on. While some women are "good sports" about watching an occasional porno movie, most women feel repelled and angry when men take pleasure in films and pictures that reduce women to sex objects.

While men spend billions of dollars on *Playboy, Penthouse, Hustler* and other "girlie" magazines, *Playgirl,* a magazine that reduces men to sex objects, is a poor seller among women. Women relate better to male "sexy dancers" who portray a theme and provide live entertainment.

Though pornography may enhance sex for men, it has little to do with intimacy. Women are seldom interested in hard pornography in any form because it is related to violence and it turns them into victims. Hard pornography is regarded as dangerous to women because it may incite men to violent acts. Certainly, it does not make men better lovers.

How To Increase Intimacy

Women are more interested in intimacy than sex in and of itself. What can women do to increase relationship intimacy? Why ask what women can do rather than what men should do about intimacy? We would prefer women and men were equally interested in this theme but that is not the case. When variations between people are rooted in biology, culture, and habit, they are highly resistant to change.

However, both women and men want to be loved and respected. They both want to establish rapport and connections with their partners. Men are also interested in closeness, especially erotic physical closeness. They are not of the same mind when it comes to intimacy, the sharing of thoughts, feelings, and ideas of a highly personal nature. Men are not comfortable with that which makes them vulnerable. However, they are more likely to share intimacies with women than with other men.

You have learned in this chapter men express intimacy by being with women, making love to them, doing things for them, including getting ahead in the world.

When a man invites a woman to a sporting event to "share" himself with her, she may see this as an indication that he really doesn't want to be close to her. Why else would he take her somewhere with 80,000 roaring fans and then pay more attention to the game than to her? To a man, this is a way of loving. This is his version of being with others, men included. Until you understand and accept this, and realize that you have been trained to experience intimacy in a different, not a better way, you will be frustrated.

It is also necessary to understand and accept another male way of being loving and intimate: Sex. You may want to talk and share feelings to be close. He may feel closest when making love. Women typically require closeness and intimacy before they have the experience of good sex.

Women feel intimate when they talk, touch, and share their thoughts and feelings with their loved one. Work toward sharing his way of being intimate while you encourage him to understand and share your intimate thoughts and feelings.

Here are a few things to try. Begin by imagining the man in your life as he was as a little boy. He needed his parents' attention and love. This made him vulnerable to rejection. These fears are still a part of him. The next step is to recall the warm, close, loving feelings you felt toward your mate at the very beginning of the relationship. Once you integrate these images, you can redesign your view of the relationship.

The next step is to act out your feelings through words and affectionate acts without the expectation that he will reciprocate immediately. View your thoughts and acts as producing a change—in the future. Whether they bear fruit or not, you will have the satisfaction of having understood and acted appropriately.

Let him know you know that you each have different styles of being loving and intimate. Ask him to explain his to you or *show* you what he thinks of as intimate. Then explain and show him what intimacy means to you.

We tend to focus on our own needs first. However, understanding that men have their way of expressing themselves will pay dividends for both of you. It encourages an end to the war of the sexes. It stops the struggle over whose view is the right one. If he believes you are taking his needs seriously, he is likely to reciprocate. It is also important to keep in mind that this is *your* decision. It is *your* desire to change the level of intimacy in the relationship that will make a difference. (This same message and procedure is intended for men.)

Achieving intimacy is a long-term enterprise in which you are taking action to change your thinking and behavior. Keep in mind that when one person changes the other cannot stay the same. Hopefully, you'll change in mutually acceptable ways.

The next chapter will demonstrate how dependency complicates the lives of women and how they can achieve autonomy *and* *inter*dependency.

5

DEPENDENT: TO BE OR NOT TO BE

Women live with painful feelings of deprivation; with longings for care, love, acceptance, and emotional contact. Each woman in her individual life and relationships searches to fill the emptiness inside and to make peace with this powerful theme of dependency and attachment.

—Eichenbaum & Orbach

The Agony of Abandonment

In the beginning, JoAnn lost her "self" by symbiotically bonding with her husband. At the time, she was unaware of the loss of her psychic independence—in fact, it felt good to "give herself" to him. Years later, when he suggested separating, JoAnn was shocked. If he left, she had nothing, not even her "self."

As we sat together in my consulting room JoAnn, a 47–year–old school administrator, tried to maintain a sense of calm. An immaculate, elegant woman, she spoke of her difficulties in a low, well–modulated voice. Everything about her appeared measured and controlled.

While visibly calm and composed, JoAnn's inner-self was out of control, "in total chaos, screaming and crying, vibrating with anxiety," as she later put it. She came to therapy hoping to quiet her emotions and find the strength to make decisions.

JoAnn described her reaction when her husband Bill, a 46–year–old certified public accountant, informed her that he was unhappy in their marriage. "It was a horrible deja~vu. Six years ago Bill said he 'needed space' and I was dumbfounded. I later discovered he was involved with another woman, but I couldn't accept it—not that I should have. I immediately told him to get out.

"He did. In a week he was back begging for forgiveness. It was humiliating for both of us. Everyone knew what he did because I couldn't shut up. I told family, friends, my kids, and anyone else within listening range. When I let him come back I felt ashamed that I'd told everyone about our problems. I was embarrassed because everyone could see I was a spineless wimp that he was able to control with his pathetic apologies.

"And, what's more, instead of distancing myself from him six years ago, he became my life—and that's not healthy. I try not to focus so much of myself on him but I can't help it. It's like, if he smiles and likes me, I feel great but if he's grumpy or distracted, I immediately think it's my fault. My mind races: What did I do? What can I do to make him feel better?

"I've lived my life for him, doing everything I can think of to make him happy, but he's not satisfied and I'm falling apart."

JoAnn has placed herself in an impossible position with Bill. She doesn't feel happy unless he's feeling good and lets her know it. JoAnn's concentration on Bill skews the relationship and places too much power on his side of the equation.

JoAnn's mental set—"my man first and foremost"—was ground into her by both her mother and father. JoAnn was taught to believe she was a princess and would find a prince who would care for her. She was also given the message that women who think and act independently are "losers" who can't attract a man. Despite some vague, knowing, doubt that her parents' message was in her self interest, JoAnn has spent her life acting out their directives.

JoAnn was shy and had to force herself to move away from her safe but painful dependency. She was able to make the transition during a year of intense therapy. Still married, JoAnn is strengthening her separate "self" by deliberating propelling herself into sports and social activities, renewing old relationships, and developing new friendships. These activities are difficult since, as JoAnn says, "It doesn't feel natural."

For dependent women, finding sources of satisfaction apart from the marital or main relationship may be experienced as superficial and unfulfilling. But, new interests and activities are critical to a developing self. If the dependent woman's self-esteem depends on compulsively serving others' needs, she is in danger of losing herself.

If her partner decides he has more pressing interests or fails to pay proper attention to her, the dependent person usually reacts by trying to re-establish the dependency. Her partner is likely to pull further away because of the very behavior that is meant to bring him closer. Men are ambivalent about dependency. It puts a great deal of pressure on them.

Who Is Dependent?

Shy, gregarious, or somewhere in between, we all long to be loved, nurtured and cared for unconditionally by a mothering person who has our best interests at heart—just like a baby. Our needs to be cared for, wanted, and protected are primitive, basic desires that are originally satisfied by our mothers. Thereafter, we may seek out others to gratify our needs, our spouses, lovers, family members—anyone that is close to us.

What does it mean to be dependent? Even though dependency is a human condition experienced by both women and men, dependency is considered a "female" trait, synonymous with weakness. Irene Stiver (1984) defines dependency as, "A process of counting on other people to provide help in coping physically and emotionally with the experiences and tasks encountered in the world, when one (individual) has not sufficient skill, confidence, energy and/or time."

Stiver believes that the emotional component of dependency is healthy when a person feels "enhanced and empowered" as a result of counting on another for help. Women, more than men, are able to show dependency needs openly by self-disclosing. Women freely acknowledge and express emotional needs and fears, vulnerabilities, and the desire to be cared for.

Nevertheless, women are more often dependent in the *maladaptive* sense if they avoid worldly challenges, do not express opinions that may lead to conflict and disapproval, are not proactive, or shy away from opportunities for autonomy and independence.

The battered woman syndrome exemplifies the worst attributes of dependency. These women typically have no material resources of their own. They've either never had their own assets or they have turned them over to their husbands.

They are also dependent upon the abuser for their psychological and social well-being. They do not think for themselves. If their best interests are pointed out to them, they have rationalizations as to why they cannot take appropriate action. The abused woman must go through a process of becoming independent, of "finding" herself and her own voice, before she can reach interdependence.

To be *interdependent* means that each person's fate and welfare is determined by interacting fairly and cooperatively with other. Each person in the system contributes something valuable to the social unit. The improved quality of life is a function of mutual contributions between willing parties.

When inequality exists, you can be sure that all parties are under strain. The dominant party struggles to maintain an advantage while the subordinate person attempts to minimize their losses. Here's an account of how dependency created problems in a relationship:

> Ann's friendly, carefree manner did not fit her view of herself as a "36–year–old dull stay–at–home." In an

unusually soft voice during a consultation, Ann said, "It's slowly dawned on me how dependent I am. I've become aware of how little control I have over my own life. My husband, Jack, is my caretaker."

He care–takes you?

"He handles the finances, always goes grocery shopping with me, makes the decisions when it comes to buying furniture—even arranging it—and he always has opinions about anything I do, say, or wear."

Have you objected?

"I guess—I'm afraid if I make an issue of it, he wouldn't love me and he would leave. I seldom challenge him to see what would happen." She paused several seconds then said, as if she was taking stock of her life, "But, you know, I've gradually insisted on going to the store alone. I know that sounds like nothing, but to me it's a big thing. When he questions me about why I bought something, I've started saying, 'I wanted to' or something like that. I don't scramble to make excuses like I used to. Instead, Jack makes excuses for me. He says something like, 'Oh, oh, it must be PMS time.'

"I was scared to tell him to his face, 'this is what I think, period!' But, it's funny, if I'm definite about what I've done or what I think, he gets off my back.

"Still, the next day it's a struggle all over again. I don't know if I can keep it up. I walk in his shadow while most of the time I'm afraid of my own. I think Jack likes it that way."

Ann attended college while living at home, wasn't employed, seldom socialized, and was taken care of by her parents. While dating Jack, her very first boyfriend, she felt as if her dream had come true; Jack freed her from her parents' grasp. It felt like a natural transition to Ann.

Jack was comfortable with the arrangement, too. He wanted a dependent person to enhance his self-esteem and sense of security. What could be better than a woman without resources who wouldn't be too demanding? A requirement for masculinity is the ability of the male to provide for his family. Jack could feel right about his role because men substitute giving and doing for intimacy and emotional closeness.

But, dependency is a two edged sword: It both integrates a couple and creates difficulties for them. Men want to experience themselves as masculine, self–sufficient, and independent. This means they must find someone who depends upon them. Ann's beautiful dream became a nightmare because she transferred her dependency from parents to husband.

Dependency Leads to Vulnerability

Women are reared to desire closeness and intimacy with others. They are groomed for dependency. They come to need it. When their emotional dependency is added to their reliance on others for material well-being women are in an especially vulnerable position. Unfortunately, dependency does not carry high value or esteem with it (Stiver, 1984).

As therapists, we frequently counsel with women who are dissatisfied with their marriages but they are stalemated because they are so dependent upon the male emotionally and financially. They settle miserably into an unsatisfactory life since divorce would mean a significant loss of life style. How do women arrive at this state in life where they must choose between their happiness, growth, and economic comforts?

Actually, dependency is natural to both women and men since they spend so many years as dependent children. Boys are groomed from an early age to believe that providing for a family is a *rite of passage* to become a man. Boys are encouraged to be active and adventuresome while girls are taught to be reactive and passive. Women learn to want a home and children even if they choose to have a career. (Ninety percent of all young women indicate they eventually want to have children.)

Early conditioning resonated into the adult lives of Joni and Fred:

> Appearing shy and apprehensive Joni walked into her first counseling session with eyes downcast. Small boned, blonde and pretty Joni, 37, presented herself like a child beginning school. She said, "I don't know where to begin. Would you ask me some questions?"
>
> *How did you feel about coming to therapy?*
>
> "It was hard. It took a long time to make the phone call."
>
> *It's a hard decision to make and difficult to carry through. Talking to a stranger about your life isn't easy.*
>
> "I know. But, I knew I had to do it," Joni said, and the ice was broken. Joni spoke in short, choppy sentences while she warmed up to her task of speaking about herself. "I'm nervous all the time, especially when I'm home. I hate to be home. I have a part–time job and I love to go to work." Laughing uncomfortably she continued, "People seem to like me at work and say I do a good job.

"I don't talk about myself very often. At home my husband, Fred, is the one who does the talking, I should say bossing. He makes all the decisions. That's why I'm here." Visibly relaxing, Joni continued, "It seems like he blames me for everything. He fights with our 19–year-old daughter and then gets mad at me because I don't jump in on his side. Well, most of the time I think he's wrong—but I don't say that in front of her. I just don't agree with him."

Joni has always "let" her husband make decisions about social events, sex, money, and what should be in the family's best interests. Joni says, "Fred's in charge of sex. He wants sex every day. I refuse to have sex every day now—but I used to."

Joni and Fred were teenagers when they married. Fred became the man of the house with an "I–know-what's–best" attitude that blended in well with Joni's dependent style.

Joni fits Fred's needs perfectly since she does not assert herself nor confront his behavior. As a child, Joni developed an inner sense of confusion when she was physically and psychologically battered. She was either hit, ignored or called stupid and ugly by the adults in her household. Joni continues to doubt her thoughts and feelings but the praise she receives from her work performance has raised her self-confidence.

Growing up, Fred identified with the aggressor, his mother. Fred's mother is a dominant controlling woman who is always right, knows the answer to everything, not only for herself, but for everyone else. Fred continues to fear being dominated and is always on guard since he sees women as dangerous and emasculating. To compensate for his fears, Fred is dominant and definitive, rigidly in charge and master of his domain.

During their 20 year marriage Joni has happily worked outside the home, always part–time, to make money and get away. Her present job is the "best" she's had and she wishes it was full time to avoid the conflict at home.

Joni reports feeling "testy" with her husband and often finds herself unable to tolerate his behavior. For five years she's desired a change in her marital relationship but has been unable to take action, including talking seriously to Fred about her feelings. She's beginning to understand that as she opens the door of independence just a crack, it frightens her husband.

Fred complains bitterly about money shortages and talks about the heavy responsibility he has financing the family's lifestyle and putting a child through college. "Our house will be paid off in six months and we have no debts," Joni says. "We're in a lot better shape than most people our age. I think he's complaining just to keep me in line."

Therapy focused on Joni's immediate problems. She learned to calm herself and to make her own decisions. She learned to prepare for her husband's arguments and anger. After several months of therapy, Fred became so distressed by alterations in her behavior that he insisted on marriage counseling.

He tried to use the therapist as an ally to return Joni to her previous state of dependency. The therapist reacted with various interpretations of his need to control others. He reacted to his wife with anger and threatened to leave the marriage. When Joni held firm, Fred was faced with a choice: Change his behavior or end the marriage. He chose to work on the marriage.

Joni and Fred are working on new adaptations. Joni has her ups and downs— feeling stronger and then falling back. When she has her "ups" she feels she has rights, is a person, and will not be controlled by Fred or her old habits. Fred is coming to terms with his wife's need to grow. He's also finding that as she makes progress, she feels better and their relationship improves. He's starting to welcome the changes because it improves his life as well. He's more sensitive to his own need to control, sees the negative effects that has, and is working to abandon his bullying.

How is it that Joni and Fred are locked in this struggle over dependency and autonomy? As adults, shouldn't they have settled this issue of dependency long ago? Actually, the problem was established before they laid eyes on one another; they were trained and reinforced to be dependent and dominant as their "gender birthrights."

Training Daughters For Inequality

A crucial factor in the inequality between the sexes can be traced to the ways sons and daughters are parented and socialized. Girls have an enduring and close association with their mothers whereas these same mothers move their boys toward independence. Traditionally, girls are taught that one of their primary tasks as a female is to find a "good husband" or any husband at all. A good husband is one who will love them, provide for the family, and be a good father. Girls are taught by overt and subtle means that women must have children to fulfill their destiny.

While mothers are no longer as blatant about their daughters' need for a male, in various ways they still convey the message: "Something is missing if you are not married. To be unmarried is to be unfulfilled."

One of our clients swore she married and quickly divorced her husband to get her mother "off my back." She was tired of being "fixed up" and hassled about being single. Another client reported mixed messages from her mother. The mother made it clear that her daughters must, above all, "acquire a man." However, she never approved of any of the men her daughters dated. She also told her daughters it was important to get an education and have a career but this was secondary.

Girls grow up in families in which the mother may run the household but the father has the final say and the most power. In many families daughters experience the father devaluing the mother by criticizing and doubting the mother's decisions. If the father is abusive, the daughter becomes disturbed that mother does not defend herself or the daughter.

When a daughter sees her mother abused verbally or physically she is inadvertently set up to accept dominance and abuse in the relationships she will later form. In therapy many women ask—in reference to their mothers—"Why *did* she take it? Why *does* she take it?" While she is both empathic with and angered by her mother's acceptance of abuse, she also identifies with and may accept her father's perceptions and attitudes toward the mother.

Eichenbaum and Orbach (1981) point out that pressure is put on the mother-daughter relationship in four ways:

1. Daughters are trained to be givers, to be unselfish and to develop antennae for others' emotional needs. A daughter must develop her self–esteem based on these traits although they point her toward submission and dependency.

2. Daughters grow up to expect nurturing from their mates as they received it from their mothers. However, she's unlikely to get it from her husband. The daughter has seen the inequality in her parents' relationship and accepts it in her own marriage.

3. A daughter may be relied upon by an unsatisfied mother to meet her emotional needs. In this case, the daughter is a stand–in for her father. This puts a burden on the daughter and makes it difficult for her to achieve autonomy.

4. Having been taught by generations of women before her not to want or demand too much the mother resigns herself to her fate and teaches her daughter the same lesson. The message is, "Be careful, you are not free, you are a weakling in the world."

There is likely to be confusing ambivalence in the mother's messages. She may tell her daughter to be all she can be but at the same time imply that the daughter must scale back her expectations. Her attitude is not unlike

that of the minority mother who teaches her
sons they live in a dangerous world. She lets
them know that if they are too assertive they
may lose their freedom or their lives.

Motivated by fear for her daughter's
happiness and welfare, the traditional mother
paradoxically diminishes daughter by teaching
them to reduce their expectations. Candace, a
19–year–old college student, provides us with
a clear example of how discriminatory
attitudes toward boys and girls encourage the
female into inferiority and dependency.

> Candace attended college full time, worked part time
> and lived at home with her parents. Because her mother
> also worked, Candace did most of the housework while
> her brother did none. When the lawn had to be cared for,
> Candace's job was to rake and bag the grass after her
> brother mowed. Her complaints about the difference in
> work load between her and her brother were ignored by
> both parents.

Candace and other girls learn they must
take over the unpleasant and routine work in
the household and defer to the males in the
household. This differential in status between
boys and girls not only prepares women for
subservience but also lays the ground work for
later resentment. Many men complain their
wives are angry and shrill about not being
helped in the home.

Although a father is an important
influence in a little girl's life, he is often
perceived as a powerful figure who comes and
goes. He operates on the edge of the little
girl's world. A father who takes an active role

and is a central figure in his daughter's life is much likelier to have a high achieving daughter. One study of women who are officers in businesses found that the fathers of these women treated them just as they would a "capable son." Fathers took daughters to work with them, taught them about business, and expected them to achieve.

Men's Ambivalence About Autonomy and Dependency

By definition, men are not supposed to be dependent. Masculinity excludes dependence. Men are in control as the breadwinners with few emotional needs. Yet, men are allowed and are expected to be dependent on the mother/lover/wife to understand and manage the emotional undercurrents in their lives.

Women are taught to depend on men to provide structure in the world. Simultaneously, they want men to be sensitive, caring, emotional and sharing. They find it hard to get both needs met by one person.

Women often choose men who will be good providers to enhance their security and provide them with high status. At the same time, women seek men who can *connect* with them, who can be open and vulnerable and disclose intimate thoughts and feelings. Alas, these qualities are seldom found in young men.

For their part, men expect women to be emotional and feminine, not competent or powerful. They make great demands upon women and expect women to do their bidding, but they don't want women to compete with them. Men who desire close relationships are also in a double bind. They are expected to be independent and competent while meeting their own and their partner's emotional needs. When they show their sensitive side, as Bruce did, they may be labeled "wimps."

Bruce, 42, came into therapy suffering from depression. Unusually handsome and well dressed, he described himself as a confident and positive person, until recently, when he realized his wife did not respect him.

Historically, Bruce said he was an adventurous, upbeat young man who had gone to work for an engineering firm right out of college. A year later he was unhappy with his job and used all of his savings to go to Europe with a friend. He stayed until his money ran out. When he returned, he found a sales job that allowed him more freedom and a higher salary than engineering.

About this time he met Jane, an executive secretary. They courted for two and a half years. Jane decided she wanted to be married and gave him an ultimatum: "Marry me now or lose me." He felt the time was right, yet he was not deeply in love with her. In fact, he was casually seeing other women.

Shortly after the marriage, Jane wanted Bruce to talk to her more, but he felt she always pulled at him, wanting too much. This led to arguments and hard feelings. His response was to be away from home as often as possible. He convinced himself he needed to work harder to further his career.

Bruce accepted jobs with the enticement of more money and responsibility but each required moving the family. Jane was expected to run the home while he "brought home the bacon." His last career move changed their relationship. Bruce's company moved him to Colorado only to shut down the office six months later and terminate his position.

Jane berated him for taking the job and added that his actions and calculations showed he was not a clear thinker. Instead of defending himself against Jane's attacks Bruce became calm and passive with the realization their relationship had forever changed.

Although financially and in the eyes of the world Bruce was a good husband, earlier in the marriage he was only moderately interested in his wife and family. Now he realized the sands had shifted. Now he actively needed Jane's love. He had taken his family for granted and Jane had learned to do without him. Too late, Bruce mustered the courage to let her know how he was feeling and tried using her as a sounding board, seeking understanding and empathy. Jane was uninterested.

How did Jane go from being totally preoccupied with the relationship to relative disinterest in it?

Bruce entered the marriage as a distant, independent person. Jane wanted to be a part of Bruce's worldly life and while she wanted him to talk to her and be open, she was also trained to accept a distant male. Necessity was a part of her acceptance; she needed Bruce as the family provider.

The change in Bruce's status forced the couple to face their interpersonal problems. When Bruce lost his job and self–confidence, Jane's economic and emotional dependency on Bruce decreased while Bruce's relational needs increased. As Jane became stronger, Bruce became more dependent and fearful.

Each of them struggled to understand Jane's disappointment and anger. The years of emotional distance had eroded Jane's feelings of love for Bruce. Nevertheless, she had clung to her early dream of togetherness: the family living happily ever after. When Bruce lost his job, it was the last straw. Bruce's inability to support the family dealt his ego a cruel blow. It was the last straw for Jane; if he couldn't support the family why should she put up with her situation? Bruce was devastated by Jane's reaction and felt she let him down when he needed her most. His image of himself was shattered by the loss of his job and he needed Jane's comfort and nurturing. As Bruce scrambled to find his place in Jane's life he realized that he had not been a "family man." Bruce felt helpless and hopeless as he slipped into a depression.

In therapy Bruce and Jane eventually made an adaptation and shifted into roles with more balance. Bruce was now available to hear and act on Jane's relationship desires. Jane was ready for independent status and decided to return to the world of work. Bruce continued individual therapy, made a career change and developed facets of himself he had never explored before.

As Bruce and Jane's relationship matured, they actively struggled to balance their dependency issues. As couples age, it is usual for males to become less dominant while females become more assertive.

In the early years of a relationship the male's dominance is often accompanied by a lack of emotional involvement. "Dead–ended," "thwarted," and "frustrated" are a few of the terms women use to describe life with an emotionless man. Men's emotional avoidance intensifies women's emotional dependence as they try to close the gap between themselves and their mates. Experiencing his lack of emotionality and connectedness as a *personal failing*, she may feel she is not lovable.

Men's Trade Off: Achievement For Intimacy

When a young man gains access to the outer world, he loses some touch with his inner world, especially the inner world of emotions. Blunting one's emotions is necessary to live in the competitive marketplace. The male must master his environment and himself by being competitive, being successful, splitting off his emotions to live in a man's world, and engaging in raw conflict when necessary. This diminishes the value of emotions.

Covering up events that lead to vulnerability is *de rigueur*. Frederick Buechner's (1991) father committed suicide when Buechner was ten. As a boy and as a grown man he kept this secret so tightly controlled that neither father nor suicide was mentioned in the immediate family. Recently, Buechner decided to reveal the truth and heal himself:

> It is important to tell at least from time to time the secret of who we truly and fully are...because other wise we run the risk of losing track of who we are and little by little come to accept instead the highly edited version that we put forth in the hope that the world will find it more acceptable than the real thing.

It is not uncommon for a puzzled look to come into a man's eyes if he is asked about his *feelings* or *emotions*. As clinicians, when we ask men to share their feelings we usually get a glazed look back or they discuss their thoughts.

Men pay a price for avoiding emotions and depersonalizing. True, they gain control of themselves, in part, by avoiding their emotions. "Yes, son, your dog has just been run over, but don't cry. You have to be brave." Little boys are taught that big boys don't cry if they aspire to become men. But, they cut themselves off from an extremely important dimension of any human being: feelings.

Is this constriction all bad? Whether a particular masculine or feminine trait is advantageous, depends on the context in which it occurs. To become a relative stranger to one's emotions can be helpful. Technological man must be dedicated to goal oriented behavior and must process things at great speed. Feelings could get in the way. The male trained to ignore feelings may be a more effective organizational man; he is emotionally deadened and dependent on no one. He gets the job done no matter who gets hurt or what price must be paid.

Men get their emotions under control to live with other men and for the world of work. The consequences include a trained incapacity to be tender and emotional in personal relationships with either women or men.

A *trained incapacity* means the person carries this style into all situations, even when it is not appropriate: An executive tries to run the home like the office; a military man tries to produce the same order in his home that prevails in the barracks. Likewise, a woman who is used to being the social, emotional mediator in her home has difficulty being assertive in her place of employment and leaving aside her feelings when a situation requires instrumental behavior.

The Seduction of Marriage

Although living alone is an accepted alternate life style, the vast majority of adults expect to marry at least once. If they divorce, remarriage is likelier to occur than if they never married. Why?

Men and women long for companions of the opposite sex to fulfill personal and social dependency needs. Some couples are able to meet dependency needs directly and equally. They share their hardships and pleasures while establishing a powerful, truly loving relationship.

However, the habit and the advantages of living in a household are so great some people sacrifice personal happiness and growth to maintain the structure of the marriage.

Different Approaches to Marriage and Occupation

While the lives of men and women are inextricably interwoven, for women, family is at the core of their lives; for men it's at the periphery.... For most men, work and family are distinct and separate spheres of living (Rubin, 1978, p. 109).

The implications of this difference between women and men are enormous. For example, Rubin interviewed a 20 year–old male about his dreams for the future:

When you were small, what did you think you'd be when you grew up?
Well, I didn't know what I would be, but I knew I'd work. I always knew I had to be something.
What about getting married and being a father? Did you ever think about that?
No. I never gave any thought to having a family or being a parent. I don't remember having any fantasies about getting married or having children. I don't know...I guess I just assumed a wife and kids would be in my life one day, but it wasn't anything to dream about" (p. 110).

For this young man, marriage and parenthood "...wasn't anything to dream about. For a girl, if it's not the only dream in her life, it's surely dominant" (p. 110). The imbalance here is evident. **A woman's first priority is the family and relationships whereas men see women and family as only a part of their lives.**

For a man, marriage is likelier to be what he does in addition to what he is. He values marriage and family as a *component* in his life, a component he's likely to take for granted. Primarily, he identifies himself through his occupation: computer programmer; automobile service manager; engineer; truck driver; etc. Work, not family, is his source of identity. His success or failure is gauged by what he *does* for an income and how successful he is as a provider. Whether his house is kept clean and how his children are raised, is mainly his wife's job.

The need to succeed puts pressure on men. They often displace their aggression from the job to others, as Dave did:

David and Monica were referred to us because of a pending divorce action which David opposed. David, 41, is a sales rep for several toy manufacturers. Monica, 38, is presently unemployed, although she has worked on and off as a bookkeeper. David is often abusive verbally and sometimes physically to his wife and children. In therapy he tries to dismiss the abuse as unimportant by claiming he has "reasons" for being the way he is. He strongly resents our concentration on his abusiveness.

Over the past 13 years, he has moved his family from state to state, the result of three successive job losses. This was stressful for him and his abusiveness increased beyond Monica's limits of tolerance. When she refused to sign over some of her property to him, he threatened to divorce her. Much to his surprise and consternation, she promptly filed for divorce.

Now he is willing to stop being violent. *Now* he is willing to go into therapy. *Now* he is willing to re–examine the abusive parts of his relationship with his three children. In short, now that his family is coming apart and he can no longer ignore the problem, he wants a quick fix for the problem.

Monica has put the divorce on hold while she and her husband are in marriage counseling but she is adamant that David must change. Our impression is that David wants to calm his wife and stabilize the marriage as a temporary concession so he can concentrate on his main interest—his new business.

Men are likely to expect their woman to be a part of the team that aids their career goals. Daniel Levinson's findings confirm the emphasis that men place on their work (1978, p. 83). He studied men from different social classes and found that from the male point of view, relationships with women are subordinate to their occupational growth: [For the man]...

> entering the adult world...occupation and marriage and the family are the components likeliest to be given central importance. One task is to choose and follow an occupational direction that permits him to define important parts of himself. A related task is to form a marital relationship with a wife who supports his aspirations and is ready and able to join him on his journey.

The male's orientation to the world, which focuses upon the development of his own interests—occupational performance and avocations, not relationships—gives him an enormous advantage in life. It results in substantial financial compensation, an established place in the world, a predictable life, and a concrete understanding of his identity. Moreover, if there is a divorce, he retains his earning power; he may suffer emotionally but he will maintain or improve his lifestyle while his ex-spouse and the children will suffer a decline in their standard of living.

Still, there are costs associated with these benefits. While the male's time and energy are consumed by his quest for status, it stunts his personal growth and keeps him from developing sensitivity to other's needs. He may become distant from his children and never develop intimate relationships. But, he may not care about personal growth and sensitivity. If you don't know what it is, you don't miss it.

One of our female clients recently phoned to ask, what for her, was a critical question:

Can a 64–year–old man who is otherwise a good person, ever learn to communicate?

She reported her husband held friends and acquaintances spellbound with his talk but had almost nothing to say to her. When she asked about his feelings, she received a short answer with no elaboration. He was successful in being hale, hearty, and well-met but on a one–to–one basis he was poor at communication. Both of his previous wives thought so too.

However, he expressed no dissatisfaction with his life. If his wife's decision to stay with him depends upon his changing from relating at a relatively superficial level to a deeper one, she will soon be divorced.

Compulsive Giving and Loving

Whereas many men are detached from women and the family because they over-focus on work, there are women so needy to give that they *insist* on it no matter how little the receiver deserves or desires their offerings. When caring is *forced* on someone, they are likely to perceive it as aggression or meaningless. (This compulsive caring was the subject of a book aptly titled, *Women Who Love Too Much*, 1985.)

A compulsive need to give is illustrated by Sally's approach to her fiancee's children:

Marv, 51, asked Sally, 46, to marry him but he wanted to delay the wedding for several years. He had adult and adolescent children living with him and felt a duty to them. Secretly, he felt he could not simultaneously husband Sally *and* parent his children the way he wanted to. Sally had already announced she wanted to be his children's "friend."

Sally not only wanted to be close, she *had* to be close. She felt left out when she was discouraged from assisting Marv's daughter plan her graduation party. Marv's daughter saw Sally as an interloper, a competitor for her father's love, and as pretender to the throne of "Real Mother."

Sally had much to give but she gave it as though compelled to give it. Such giving is akin to a junkie needing a fix: If she can't have what she craves she goes into withdrawal. Sally threatened to leave the relationship and began a campaign against the children. It was at this point Marv and Sally sought couple therapy.

We helped Sally become aware of the driven nature of her desire to be close. If she is dependent upon others to receive her love to feel O.K. about herself, then she no longer controls her own fate. You cannot compel or trick others into loving you. Eventually, she saw that she was engaging in self–defeating behavior.

Slowly, she stopped grilling Marv about his children and what they were doing. She no longer offered her opinion about how well or poorly he parented them. Sally also carved out a life of her own because her romance with Marv was largely a weekend relationship. When he phoned, she returned his calls when it was convenient for her to do so instead of rearranging her own priorities to be ever–available to him. Marv felt uncomfortable when Sally changed her behavior, but both felt better when he finally understood and accepted her distant stance.

A woman's strength, emotional sensitivity, also makes her vulnerable. Being sensitized to your own and others' feelings can be exhausting and confusing if it is not reciprocated or if it is regarded—as it often is by men—as prying or "pathological sensitivity." A man may regard a woman's need to be involved as overbearing, an unwelcome intrusion, or a demand for reciprocity that he is unwilling or unable to give.

Women are in danger of being abandoned emotionally and physically by the very men they choose to fill their needs. Women have a precious quality in their caring; they need to use it judiciously.

What's A Woman To Do?

Females of all ages live in a world of connection where, according to Deborah Tannen (1990), women "negotiate complex networks of friendship, minimize differences, try to reach consensus, and avoid the appearance of superiority, which would highlight differences" (p. 26). Contrast this with a man's world which is more dependent on power than on compromise and empathy.

Women and men also have different styles of communication. Words are a woman's path to intimacy. Women tend to agonize over what they've said and mull over what others have said, analyzing and interpreting. A woman is careful about speaking out or speaking up for fear that she may hurt some one's feelings by saying the wrong thing. A female friend, describing a phone conversation with her brother in another state, told him she was ending the conversation. She later called him back because she was afraid she had hurt his feelings by ending their talk without a suitable explanation.

Females present their ideas tentatively, particularly when speaking to men, whereas men's words are statements that convey pragmatic, concrete ideas. Men are satisfied with the essence of what they want to communicate; details don't matter that much. They're more than a little annoyed by women who remember every detail of what they've said and hold them to it.

Women remember what was said and by whom. Words seem to have more significance and meaning to women; it's one of their sources of power. When men speak they do so in a dominating, definitive, "here's the truth" style. Male definiteness can be a shriveling experience for women when their own thoughts are treated as inconsequential.

Another powerful form of psychological dependency inherent in a woman's marital status is the agreement that she's responsible for how well family members manage their lives. In this sense she lives vicariously, dependent upon others for her sense of success. Her status depends upon how well others do. If the kids aren't up to standard in their behavior or performance, it's the mother who takes the blame.

Women are the specialists for the inner world of the family. That is their area of expertise. Women make sure others are happy, mature properly, and have a proper emotional environment in which to thrive. *If a woman is to be happy, others must be happy first.*

Men are assigned responsibility for the outside world; women have responsibility for the inner world of the family. He's the *world-maker*; she's the *home--maker*. Being a world-maker has a connotation of being powerful whereas *"home-maker"* implies a role of service to others.

While a woman has power in the home, at the same time she has "powerless responsibility" rather than social power (Young–Eisendrath and Wiedmann, 1990, p. 22). In other words, a mother is responsible for her children and takes responsibility for their actions in spite of the fact that genetic programing, personality factors, environment and peers are equally powerful determinants of a child's outcome.

Although women are assigned responsibility for the family and relationships, women's satisfaction does not highly correlate with care giving. Studies of marriage and mothering show high levels of dissatisfaction and distress. A study of pleasure (finding life enjoyable) and mastery (feeling important and worthwhile) found that women need to understand and develop both aspects of well–being to feel good about themselves and their lives (Baruch, Barnett, and Rivers, 1983). The most significant findings are as follows:

1. A woman who works hard at a challenging job is doing something positive for her mental health.

2. Marriage and children do not guarantee well–being for a woman. Being without a

man or being childless does not guarantee depression or misery.

3. Doing and achieving are at least as important to the lives of women as are relationships and feelings. If that side of a woman's life is neglected, her self–esteem is endangered (p. 29).

Not surprisingly, marriage benefits husbands more than wives (Bernard, 1972). Married men are happier than married women. The Baruch, Barnett and Rivers study revealed that challenging paid work accompanied by supportive egalitarian relationships with men contributes most strongly to a woman's sense of well–being in adult life. These findings have been supported in more recent studies to determine which gender profits most from marriage.

Developing self interests and close relationships help to balance a woman's life. A woman needs her own time, her own space, and her own life. To be totally dependent on a male and/or the family for fulfillment, is risky— too many eggs in one basket. Personal autonomy needs to be balanced with the obligations and rights that go along with relationships. Men, on the other hand, are viewed as naturally independent, a condition of their gender, their birthright. Can both genders create more balance in their needs for commitment and autonomy?

Women Can Combine Dependency and Autonomy

Presently, women as well as men are expected to be independent and career oriented. However, despite all the talk about women breaking through traditional barriers, women either do not work, work part–time, or work to keep the family afloat financially. More women are developing careers but they have a long way to go to catch up with men.

Most women say they would like a career along with successful relationships and a happy family (Halcomb, 1979). For women, timing is a problem. The phase of life devoted to forming relationships and establishing families is also the period of life when career oriented individuals devote almost exclusive attention to developing their careers.

Women in the workforce also carry the primary responsibility for home and children. These are time and energy restrictions to career development. Because women are expected to be home-makers, they find it difficult to "selfishly" take the time necessary to acquire vocational skills. However, without work skills, being cared for financially fosters a child–like dependency. Women without their own assets are in danger of losing their financial support through separation, divorce, death, or their partner's loss of employment.

A male may be independent financially but simultaneously trapped in his job due to family responsibilities. Ironically, a woman may have opportunities to change her life style while she's financially dependent. If she's being supported and has flexible time, she can use this as an opportunity to train or retrain herself in a chosen occupation.

While males take their careers seriously, women are groomed to care for others. The result of the choice between a "pure" lifestyle of home-maker or a career creates consider role conflict for women. Either in or out of the job market, women are plagued with guilt. If a woman opts to stay at home, she thinks, "I'm at home with the kids and should be contributing financially." At work she worries, "I should be at home with the children." Too many roles—mom, homemaker, and career person—are fragmenting. About 50 percent of women with children under five are now in the workforce.

A man's life rarely changes dramatically when he marries and has children; his major role persists: breadwinner. A woman's life changes drastically once she commits to a family. By the time she's fulfilled these duties she's not likely to have the same seniority in an occupation that men have.

Women's intermittent employment patterns put them at a disadvantage. Following high school or college graduation, most women get jobs. However, once they marry and get pregnant, their employment is interrupted. If they leave the workforce, they will never fully make up the difference between themselves and the men and women who maintained continuous employment. Women's jobs are viewed simultaneously as necessary to shore up the family income but unimportant as a serious career. Women are more prone to have "jobettes," men have careers.

Nevertheless, being able to generate income is critical for a woman's self esteem, growth, security and development. Monetary rewards and an interesting career are confidence builders.

Four Differences Between Women and Men

1. Married men feel **independent;** married women feel **dependent.** Marital dependency is seductive and may not fulfill female expectations of material security and relationship satisfaction.

2. Men and women have **different** approaches to marriage and occupation. Females experience their primary task as focusing on marriage and family. Males experience their primary task as the support of the family through their occupation.

3. Men see themselves as **independent** as a result of family and cultural training; dependency needs are hidden.

4. Women experience **career confusion** because of conflicts between dependence and independence. Competition and instrumental (emotionless) behavior,

more suitable in the work place, do not come as "naturally" to women.

People have conflicting desires to be both dependent and independent. The child within wants to be held, comforted, cared for and nurtured. Simultaneously, the adult within us wants to be autonomous. Family life puts these two forces to a severe test.

With an understanding of our culture, the effects of socialization and the differences between women and men, both sexes can better fashion an accommodation of their dual needs for autonomy and dependency.

The next chapter deals with how much of women's and men's difficulties are due to heredity v. personality. There are innate differences between the sexes but these differences can enhance relationships once we understand how to use them creatively and positively.

BIOLOGY AND PERSONALITY AS FACTORS IN GENDER PROBLEMS

During the Senate Judiciary Committee's October 1991 investigation of Anita Hill's sexual harassment complaints against Clarence Thomas, one Senator could not believe that one of Hill's friends (then testifying) had not offered her *advice* about the alleged harassment. The friend explained (to no avail) that Anita Hill was only in need of a "sympathetic ear" so the friend did not offer her *advice*. The Senator could not comprehend this. Presumably, any man would give advice to any woman who had a *problem*.

The Senate Judiciary Committee's behavior in the Thomas-Hill Hearings demonstrated the width of the gender gap. Because the male Senators' inability to grasp women's issues was so clearly demonstrated, a strong movement began to elect more women to the Senate. It succeeded: we now have six women in the Senate. A year after the Hill-Thomas Hearings a majority of people give serious consideration to Ms. Hill's allegations.

A culture which has institutionalized sexism as one of its building blocks will not easily rid itself of discrimination against women. Moreover, the differences between the sexes are both learned and genetically determined.

This makes it harder to get rid of sexism. The authors argue that no matter how the genders differ, there is no justification for discrimination. However, the differences, whatever their source, need to be understood and respected when they are legitimate. This Chapter will review gender differences and help us make sense of the difficulties which crop up between the sexes. Gender variations range from those that are biologically based to those that are learned to those which flow from personality and individual experiences in structured settings. When these differences come into play in the interactions between women and men, they can cause problems, some of them severe.

The Role Of Biology In Gender Problems

Is anatomy—as Freud proclaimed—destiny?

Jan Morris (1974), born and raised as a male, realized as an adult he was actually a female. Despite the fact that he was anatomically a male and regarded by others as male, he *experienced himself* as a woman. To correct this disparity between how he was socially defined and how he felt inside, he decided to live fully as a woman and to have sex change surgery and hormone treatments.

After his transformation, Morris was in a unique position to report on the extent and nature of the differences between women and men:

We are told that the social gap between the sexes is narrowing but I can only report that having, in the second half of the twentieth century, experienced life in both roles, there seems to me no aspect of experience, no moment of the day, no contact, no arrangement, no response, which is not different for men and women. The very tone of voice in which I am now addressed, the very posture of the person next in the queue, the very feel in the air when I entered a room or sat at a restaurant table, constantly emphasized my change of status (p. 148).

How much of the experience of those who undergo sex change operations is due to learned behavior as opposed to genetics and biology? It is difficult to say. Does biology dictate behavior? There's some evidence that it does. For example, studies of identical twins have provided valuable insights into the influence of biology on behavior and personality.

Dr. Thomas Bouchard and his colleagues at the University of Minnesota studied identical twins (two humans with the same genetic code). The researchers found that identical twins raised apart are often alike in their personalities and intelligence—almost as similar as identical twins raised together. This establishes the powerful role of biology in human behavior. Other twin researchers argue about the details of Bouchard's methods and findings but agree, based on their own research that heredity influences intelligence and personality. Indeed, hundreds of studies support the influence of heredity on behavior.

Left open is the question of whether women and men have, in effect, different heredities. If this is the case, we should be able to see some differences between the sexes that are related to biology. Likewise, women should be more similar to women and men to men in their behaviors. Let's review some of the differences that have been established between the sexes.

Brain Physiology and Function

It is true that the average woman and man differ in strength, weight, height, and speed. However, aren't their brains identical? Not quite.

Brain researchers (Levy, 1976, 1981; Levy and Reid, 1976) speculate that male brains are more "lateralized" than female brains. This means a male's two brain hemispheres tend to control certain functions independently whereas a female's hemispheres are more *inter*dependent.

There is support for the lateralization theory. If a male suffers brain damage to the left hemisphere's language centers, he is likely to have permanent difficulty with speech (aphasia). He may not be able to say what he wants in a logical order or even recognize the meaning of familiar words. If brain damage happens to the right hemisphere, he is more apt to suffer a loss of visual–spatial abilities.

In contrast, when women suffer brain damage to either side of the brain they usually do not show a specific loss of abilities associated with one or the other hemisphere (Inglis and Lawson, 1981). This suggests that women's brains are formed in a way that allows more communication between the left and right hemispheres and that there are important consequences that flow from this difference.

A study by Sandra Witelson, a neuropsychologist at McMaster University Medical School in Hamilton, Ontario, was based on the fact that the *corpus callosum*, the fibers connecting the left and right hemispheres, is larger in women than men. The corpus callosum is a means by which communication between the right and left hemispheres of the brain takes place.

Witelson wanted to know if this difference in brain physiology between the sexes would be reflected in their aptitudes or behavior since the female connection is 40 percent larger than the male's. Would this difference be reflected in behavior?

To find out, Witelson studied two hundred right–handed boys and girls by placing unusual objects in both their right and left hands while they were blindfolded. Then the objects were mixed with many others in a box. The subjects, still blindfolded, were challenged to find their objects among those in the box. Girls were able to find the objects they'd held in either hand but boys were accurate in identifying only those held in their left hands.

The conclusion: Boys' sensory perception was limited to one hemisphere whereas girls utilized both.

We still cannot say with certainty how much culture and opportunity affect performance. We do know that some differences may be due to brain physiology. Variations between the sexes that are genetically based need to be studied, understood and appreciated.

Physical Differences Between The Sexes

Clearly, women and men are physically distinct. Should these variations be translated into political or economic disadvantages for either sex? Of course not. Nevertheless, real differences exist. According to Tannenbaum (1989), some of the differences are:

1. Young girls draw people first; young boys draw objects.
2. Boys are likelier than girls to be left–handed, nearsighted and dyslexic (more than three to one) and hyper–active.
3. Male's eyes are more sensitive to light and they have better daylight vision. But, eight percent of men have difficulty perceiving colors whereas only half of one percent of women have this difficulty.
4. Women's joints are looser than men's allowing women to be more flexible and limber.
5. Males' hands are larger and the male thumb is as much as twenty times stronger than the female's.
6. Female lips are stiffer than male lips.

7. Female skin is more sensitive to the touch than male skin; females have more nerve endings on their skin. Male skin is thicker and less likely to bruise

8. Men have an average of 15% body fat, women average 23%. Men are 40% muscle whereas women are 23% muscle.

9. Male body temperature is 98.6 degrees with little variance whereas female body temperature may vary three to five degrees from 98.6

10. Women have a better sense of smell than males.

11. The upper body of men is stronger than the upper body of women.

12. Men have twice the arm strength of women.

13. The wider female pelvis makes them less efficient at running and climbing ladders.

Are any of these differences important? Strength is a difference that matters. But, isn't it true that in modern society physical strength is irrelevant because machines do our work? In fact, women can substitute machine power for strength and do just as well as men.

When it does come down to muscle power, women are sometimes at a disadvantage. For example, an Army study estimated that half of all enlisted women were assigned jobs too physically demanding for them. A 1987 Marine Corps study found that barely half of the women Marines could throw a hand grenade far enough *to avoid killing themselves.* Similarly, a fire*woman* might not be able to carry a heavy person down a ladder as well as a fireman.

Women have made remarkable strides in physical conditioning. Many women can run faster than many men but most men can run faster than most women. Today's female Olympian runs faster than the male Olympians of thirty or forty years ago. Excellent women runners are not as fast as excellent male runners but women are lowering their running time faster than men are. To be as fast as men, women's anatomy must approximate men's; the swiftest women are narrow–hipped and are physically similar to male athletes in other ways, perhaps even genetically.

Want proof? Open a runner's magazine and look at the body configuration of female runners. Not one of them will have the body type of the stereotypical woman. With few if any exceptions, each of them will look more like a male runner. When we blocked out the obvious sex indicator's such as hair length, people usually guessed that the figure, actually a woman's, was a man's. Women who are conditioned for running have fewer curves, including small breasts and narrow hips, due to their low proportion of body fat.

Women are better than men at cold water swimming and potentially are superior at running distances more than 100 miles. This advantage is based on fat reserves and metabolism.

Of course, some women are stronger than some men. But, the same average differential applies. Men are usually stronger than women and the difference is biologically determined.

Men have more muscle and are therefore stronger in most ways. There's little to argue about here. It is doubtful that a woman will ever win an open competition of heavy lifting. Women do excel at fine motor activities and therefore might make superior surgeons. If women performed more surgery, perhaps patients would not have so many collapsed lungs and other problems due to fine motor coordination and slips of the scalpel.

Should these biologically based strength differentials affect the social and political relationships of the sexes? Ideally, no. But in practical terms women are well-advised to take heed of a man's greater strength and willingness to use it. Men defer to other men's physical power so why shouldn't women? Strength and rape are correlated. Women would do well to respect this relationship.

For example, one of our acquaintances told us about being raped by her date. She invited a man into her apartment after their evening out. Following some small talk and a kiss, he began forcibly to remove her clothes. She protested but, since he seemed out of control and she feared he would injure her, she allowed him to undress her.

She submitted to sex because she was afraid to resist. After the rape he settled in for the night. She was afraid to ask him to leave. In the morning he got up in a cheery mood, dressed, made some small talk, had breakfast, kissed her, said he'd call her later, and left.

Once he was gone she phoned him in a rage. She vented her anger, disgust and hatred for what he'd done. *He was shocked!* In no way did he interpret the previous night's "love making" as forced. He could not believe that she considered herself to have been raped. He wanted to come right back to her house and straighten out their misunderstanding! She declined his generous offer.

A man's strength makes a difference not only physically but mentally. A woman's options may be dramatically affected by her knowledge that the man is stronger and could injure her if he chose to. However, you might be surprised to learn that women initiate violence against men about as often if not more often than men attack women. But, you would not be surprised to learn that men do more physical damage. Whether they attack first or retaliate, they are more dangerous to life and limb.

Can Women Handle Stress?

Women and men handle stress in very different ways. Endocrinologists believe that women respond better to stress because of female hormones and that men suffer more damage because of the male hormone, testosterone. Why?

The male reaction to stress is the same as it was when primitive man was threatened by a saber-toothed tiger: The body is flooded with hormones to prepare for immediate danger and flight, freeze, or fight. Women seem slower to respond to stressful situations and have less of a surge of blood pressure and stressful hormones. Men are suited for defense and attack through the quick mobilization of their energies but this in itself is costly to the body when it is frequently repeated.

Psycho–social factors also play a big role in stress reactions. Women may have a different perception of which situations are threatening. For example, women show much less stress than men when asked to solve an arithmetic problem (*U.S. News & World Report*, 1991).

Marianne Frankenhaeuser (1982) studied college students in Finland to determine their levels of stress during and immediately after an exam. She found the cost was high for females. Females reported more intense negative feelings and general discomfort than did males. Simultaneously, the women did not experience the sense of success and satisfaction that was common for the males.

Aggression

> Bev said, "I do everything at home, and have to keep track of everything that needs to be done. If Bob lifts a hand, I have to point it in the right direction. I resent it. I am angry about it. Bob's only regular task is feeding the cats, and last Sunday he went into a hissy fit about that."
>
> Bob said, "I hate cats. She knows that and still I end up with a job related to cats. I can't win. If I take charge and do something around the house, she second guesses me. If I tell her I've done something, like clean the toilets, which I figure will make her happy, she still has an attitude: 'It's your toilet too, she says.' I'm supposed to do things but never mention it. I feel I have to mention what I do or she pays no attention, gives me no credit. I'm sick of her attitude."

While Bob was talking, tears began running down Bev's cheeks, and she was patting him on the leg in an attempt to pacify him. Bob was obviously angry as he pounded the arm of the chair.

As the session proceeded both of them calmed down and began to look at their respective behavior. Bob's aggressive stance, which moved Bev to tears, was his way of maintaining control and dealing with his wife's more subtle aggression.

Are men more aggressive than women? In most cultures boys receive more rewards and less punishment for aggressive behavior than do girls. This encourages male aggression. Boys in different cultures learn to fight in different ways for different reasons. This is clear evidence that aggressiveness is learned and shaped.

Boys not only learn to fight, they learn rules about fighting "fairly": "Pick on someone your own size"; "Stop when the other person gives up"; etc. American manliness discourages fighting with those who are smaller or weaker if one is to avoid the label, "bully."

Many parents believe that boys should fight back and defend himself when attacked. Thus, males are encouraged by their peers and parents to be aggressive, to the point of violence. Is this inevitable? Is it related to hormones?

American and European research shows that boys are more active than girls and they engage in more rough–and–tumble play. Testosterone levels are correlated with the high general level of activity and of aggressiveness in males.

In other cultures, such as the Kung San, women work hard and travel long distances. They are just about as active and very nearly as rough as boys. Blurton–Jones and Konner (1973) suggest that boys and girls learn how active and aggressive to be. Western Industrial culture teaches girls, but not boys, to be passive.

Is testosterone a key factor in male aggression? Some violent men, who began raping or murdering in their teens, have elevated circulating testosterone. However, testosterone variations in normal men appear "...to be strongly modulated by psychosocial factors" (Benderly, 1987, p. 200). Activity, in short, can elevate hormones. However, testosterone must be there first, in some basic quantity, to be activated. No matter how much women exercise or aggress, they won't reach the testosterone levels of equally active and aggressive males.

Hormones, genetics, cultural prescription, individual variations, learning, and situation all determine the nature of aggression. It is also true that men in virtually all known cultures are more violent than women. The male tendency toward violence is something that both women and men must consider and learn to control.

Women, Hormones, and Behavior

Testosterone shapes some male behavior just as estrogen plays an important role in the lives of women. There's evidence that men respond to the ebb and flow of their hormones and so do women. Some women have little or no mood or behavioral change during monthly menstrual cycles while a few are debilitated both physically and emotionally. These women and their families come to dread "that time of the month." A small percentage of women become virtually "psychotic" as their monthly cycle approaches the menses.

The vast majority of women experience some degree of unpleasant emotional and physical discomfort during the menstrual cycle. These disturbances range from mild cramps and mild depression to—in the case of a few women—the urge to kill and the fear that they will.

When severe symptoms accompany menstruation they are referred to as PMS, "premenstrual syndrome," a term coined by a male physician. Couples should frankly discuss the difficulties that arise before and during menstruation and decide how they will deal with them.

Identifying the pattern and pre-planning their reaction works well for both parties. We know of one couple that sends the wife to a hotel of her choice during her darkest moods and the husband takes care of the children until she feels herself again. At times she's had the thought that she might harm her children.

If there is a negative change in mood and behavior, it is best to identify it as a normal consequence of hormonal cycles rather than mistake it as solely a relationship problem. If medical consultation and treatment doesn't relieve the problem, it is important for the couple to develop their own remedy.

If a woman has been trained to believe that she is out of control during her "time," and uses this as an excuse to be abusive or helpless, it will be damaging to the relationship. It also hurts a woman's self-esteem and credibility. She needs to be able to have her feelings without those feelings becoming self– and relationship–destructive.

There is controversy about whether or not women's moods are actually affected by menstruation. A counter explanation is that menstrual difficulties are a self–fulfilling prophecy: if one believes that one will feel bad during the menses, one will.

Your authors believe that physiological changes can be accompanied by emotional experiences and these can be conditioned by culture. The signals sent by hormonal changes are subject to interpretation and therefore, are potentially under the control of the perceiver. If you feel emotional, anxious, or angry, hormonal changes may be a partial explanation. However, it is counter productive to use "that time" as a license to engage in unkind, even nasty, remarks or behavior.

Couples can control the accompaniments of menstruation whether they're physical or social. No matter how much the hormones affect moods, how one *interprets* these experiences is optional. This is true for both the male and female. Her moods that are hormonally driven should receive at least the same consideration as his moods which may be caused by hard work and stress.

Which Is the Weaker Sex?

From conception onward females have an advantage over males: Between 130 and 150 males are conceived for every 100 females but fewer male conceptions result in a birth. More males than females die or are killed during infancy, youth and adulthood. By the age of 20 there are only 98 males per 100 females. Thereafter the mortality of males steadily creates a higher ratio of women to men. Among people 65 and older only 68 men survive for every 100 women.

When it comes to health and longevity, women have an advantage—at least in our society and for now. In 1900 American women's life expectancy was 48 years to men's 46. By 1986 women's life expectancy had increased to 78 and men's to 71.

As women take on male behaviors and habits—working in hazardous surroundings, smoking, and indulging in stressful activities—their health and life expectancy similarly suffer. Women have more illnesses or at least report more ailments and receive more care than men. Men refuse to acknowledge their many health problems and less often seek medical help during the curable and controllable stages of their diseases. This adds to their death rate. Why this disparity in health practices?

Women are trained from an early age to submit to gynecological exams; men needlessly die from prostate and colon cancer because they refuse to submit to proctological and other invasive examinations. Whether we're looking at heart attacks or lung cancer, drug use or criminal behavior, men are the "at risk" sex. The Framingham study, a twenty–seven year examination of the health of almost 6,000 women and men between the ages of 30 and 59, found approximately twice the incidence of coronary heart disease in men as in women (*U.S. News & World Report*, 1990). (Women do not receive the same level of cardiac care that men do.)

Adult women carry twice as much body fat as men whereas men have 1.5 times as much muscle and bone. This may be due to the female hormone estrogen that works to keep women's bodies in peak childbearing condition and better protects their arteries from vascular disease. Female hormones equip women with more pliable blood vessels and the ability to process fat more efficiently and safely than men (McLoughlin et al., 1988). Therefore, women have less cardio–vascular disease, at least until menopause when estrogen production drops off.

In summary, considering health and strength, the sexes are not equal. These and other sex and gender differences should be understood and respected. Sex and gender differences are no excuse for assigning sexual inferiority or superiority. Judgment simply widens the gender gap and complicate relationships.

We have reviewed some of the biological differences between the sexes that can impact negatively on gender relationships. There are also claims that women and men have different developmental paths and personalities. What is meant by this and of what significance, if any, does it have for gender relationships?

Sex, Personality, and Socialization

Personality is made up of distinctive qualities and traits that are expressed through physical and mental tendencies, patterns and activities unique to each individual. Personality traits include distinctions and behaviors labeled masculine-feminine, passive–aggressive, and introversion–extraversion. There are many more criteria used to identify personality depending on who is doing the classifying.

Personality appears to be partly hereditary and partly acquired through learning. Whether inherited or learned, personalities are shaped by culture and individual experience. Gender assignment is one of the most powerful determinants of personality.

Gendering

Through a lengthy and complex process of learning combined with heredity, we absorb and accept as a part of ourselves stereotypic male and female roles and gender self-conceptions. To demonstrate the influence of heredity, studies show that female infants between five and six months detect differences in photographs of human faces and prefer them, whereas males of the same age are somewhat more interested in objects.

Diane McGuinness (1980) reports that infant girls have a strong, early response to human faces: "Females smile and vocalize only to faces, whereas males are likely to smile and vocalize to inanimate objects and blinking lights." Children *know* by the time they are two whether they are a *boy* or a *girl*. By age three children choose toys that match society's notion of which toys are to be played with by girls and boys. Gender identification is largely irrevocable and permanent after five-years-of-age, probably much sooner.

Young children understand and can describe the differences between Mom and Dad by focusing on things like long hair and behavior. For example, "Daddies go to work and mommies cook; mommies have long hair and daddies have short hair; daddies always wear pants."

These socially designated differences between the sexes are shaped and reinforced by parents, sibs, playmates, the media, schools, etc. Once assigned to a gender it's a life long commitment. Society won't let you change your mind.

Why the Gap Between the Sexes?

Nancy Chodorow (1971) argues that much of the difference between women and men develops when boys have to give up mother and identify with males whereas girls do not have to change their gender model; they always identify with and model after the mother.

More important for our purpose is Chodorow's notion that the "feminine personality comes to define itself in *relation and connection* to other people more than masculine personality does" (pp. 43-44). This dovetails with Carol Gilligan's (1982) observation that girls develop empathy, value relationships with others, and tend to experience the feelings and needs of others as their own.

These observations by Chodorow and Gilligan are momentous because they help to explain why there is so great a difference between the sexes. It means that once children are gendered they have difficulty in relating to one another. Why? Because boys learn to be separate, but girls yearn to be *related*.

Boys learn they must *separate* themselves from mother to be male. **This may be the most important single thing they ever do in their lives**. Boys must learn separation to become men and are thereafter taught by men and women to establish distance from their own and others' feelings. In numerous ways, especially in their competition with other males, men are taught to not place high value on close relationships. There are worlds to be conquered and one cannot do this as a sentimental being. If someone needs firing or killing, well, it's a dirty job but someone has to do it.

The unfortunate consequence of gender training is that when the two sexes meet up again in adolescence girls have learned to establish intimacy and boys have learned to avoid it. Then, how is it that they get together at all if they have such different agendas?

Adolescent girls' and boys' interest in one another is partly driven by their newly flowing hormones. Raging testosterone is a major motivator when teenage boys seek out girls whereas girls want to interact on a much broader basis. Girls are interested in romance and being chosen as well as in the broader goal of mate selection. They seek togetherness. Boys are more interested in competition. How much intimacy can males and females develop?

Childhood Games, Intimacy, and Gender Distance

"He's so competitive," she said "that he'll try to race me down the slopes even though skiing is not his sport. He's barely under control but he has to get to the bottom of the hill first. It's that way in tennis, too. He goes all out to beat me so the game is no fun for me. He tries to hit the ball so hard and away from me there's no volleying; just hit and go pick the ball up at the net or the fence."

Women frequently complain they don't enjoy participating in games or sports with men because men play games to win rather than for enjoyment. Men seem unable to appreciate a sport if they don't compete. This is natural for boys and men because they try to establish their superiority in the social hierarchy through competition. A game isn't just a game; it's preparation for life and signifies where one belongs in the world.

Boys learn both the independence and organizational skills necessary for handling large groups of people and how to compete—whether they win or lose. They learn "to play with enemies and to compete with their friends—all in accordance with the rules of the game" (Lever, 1976, pp. 478-487). In short, boys' games prepare them for work but limit their skills in intimate relationships.

Recently, your authors played golf with two men at a public course. As we prepared to tee off at the fourth hole, "Clem" asked Dr. Rhodes if she'd like a golf tip; he'd noticed a defect in her swing? She firmly declined his offer but he could not stop himself from telling her what was wrong with her golf game.

Game playing is a form of "anticipatory socialization," i.e., games prepare children for their adult roles. Women and men learn different approaches to games suitable to their gender roles.

Janet Lever (1976) studied 181 fifth grade, middle class children and found that "boys play out–of–doors more often than girls; boys play more often in large and age-heterogeneous groups; they play competitive games more often; and their games last longer than girls' games" (Gilligan, 1982, p. 9). Lever sees boys' games as preparation for the work world. For example: 1. Boys continue to play even when they argue whereas girls quit the game rather than get into conflict because they want to preserve the relationship; 2. Boys' games require more skill; 3. And they are more exciting than girls' games.

According to Lever, "During the course of this study, boys were seen quarreling all the time, but not once was a game terminated because of a quarrel and no game was interrupted for more than seven minutes. In the gravest scenario, the final word was always to "repeat the play' " (p. 482).

Most of the girls Lever interviewed claimed that when a quarrel broke out, they ended the game rather than continue the dispute. Instead of establishing a set of rules for resolving disagreements as boys do, girls felt the continuation of the game was not as important as the continuation of relationships.

Piaget (1965) noted that Girls are willing to make exceptions and are more easily reconciled to innovations in their play. Girls use play to develop their sensitivity and caring for the feelings for others. Traditional girls' games like jump rope and hopscotch are turn-taking games; cooperation is the primary motivator.

Disputes requiring a referee are less likely to occur in girls' play. According to Piaget, girls have a more pragmatic attitude toward rules, considering them to be good if they preserve relationships. Otherwise, the rules can be altered to preserve the relationship if it's in danger.

Girls play in small, intimate groups, usually with best friends and in private places. This is similar to the way they will operate as adults. Their group organization is humanistic and cooperative. Girls continue throughout life to have ambivalence about competition. They do not react with the same pleasure males do when they win.

Different mind–sets are created for boys and girls that are later played out in their adult relationships. **If you understand the origin of the differences between you and the opposite sex you can discuss them and figure out ways to deal with them. Neither style is better or worse in and of itself, but if competition is used in a setting more appropriate to cooperation, there will be trouble.**

If your mate simply cannot bring himself to have fun at the games you play, do other things with him that are not competitive. Let him compete with the men. Men who insist on competing with their wives when it isn't appreciated are losing out on *doing* things with them. It is in men's interests, too, to rid relationships of unwanted competition and to promote intimacy.

How Women And Men Talk And Interpret: A Problem Area

If women and men are to respect each other's views, they will have to do better at communicating with one another. They talk to members of their own and the opposite sex in different ways and about different things.

How Each Sex Talks to Same-Sex Members

Man Talk		Woman Talk	
work	43%	children	47%
sports	42%	self–doubt	41%
future goals	28%	work	27%
self–doubt	23%	books, movies	23%
politics	21%	romance	15%
books, movies	15%	politics	10%
romance	13%	sports	8%
religion	2%	religion	2%

Adapted from *American Health Magazine* (January/February 1989 p. 11)

One of the most frequent presenting complaints in marriage and divorce counseling is that the couple "can't communicate." What prevents them from more effective communication?

Gender Talk

Socially, men are likelier to take over, direct, and interrupt conversations with women. Although it is believed women are the "talkers," in studies of actual conversations we find that **men talk more than women**. For example, one researcher found that "men tend to dominate conversations, interrupt or shift the topic to one they prefer, and...women—by adopting a questioning, tentative tone—work hard to gain men's attention," (Kohn, 1988).

Many readers will dispute our characterization of men's conversational role; they'll argue that men refuse to talk. Correct, under certain circumstances. But, this is truer when they're in an ongoing relationship and their dominance is disputed. If men don't get their way and decide not to use force, they often use withdrawal—in part to protect themselves *and* their mate from violence. Rather than argue and lose their tempers, men clam up.

In the early stages of a relationship many women experience men dominating conversation—mostly about themselves. She sits patiently, waiting her turn—which often doesn't come. "I've talked long enough," he may say. "Tell me, what do you think about ME?"

Deborah Tanen (1991) characterizes conversations between men and women as "cross-cultural." Misunderstandings arise because boys and girls grow up in "different worlds of words. Women and men talk to girls and boys differently and expect and accept different ways of talking from them."

> One of our young female clients mentioned that her husband hated to accompany her on her shopping trips to the mall. Nevertheless, she was proud of the fact that he always ended up going, hate it or not. We asked why

she thought it necessary for him to be there and she said she didn't like to be alone. Her never-fail-method for getting him to accompany her was to talk about it, pout, look depressed, talk about it *ad infinitum* until he caved in. It's safe to say that men don't understand or approve of this approach but they succumb to it. However, it's costly to the relationship.

A decade's worth of research shows that women and men in our culture use distinctive styles of speech and tend to play different roles when talking with one another. More recently, researchers have moved away from examining men's and women's language in the abstract preferring to study the actual settings—such as courtrooms and doctors' offices. Although some speech patterns are as much a function of social status as of gender, there are definite gender differences in conversational style depending on where it takes place and with whom.

Boston College sociologist Charles Derber studied the roles women and men take on in conversation and found that men often shift conversations to their preferred topics while women are more apt to respond supportively. In a study of married couples, Derber found that the wife gave more active encouragement to her husband's talk about himself while the husband "listened less well and was less likely to actively bring her out about herself and her own topics."

In fact, men often interrupt women outright and do this far more frequently than women. Candance West and Don Zimmerman, sociologists at the University of California, recorded two–party conversations (1977). When men spoke with men, or women with women, there were few interruptions and those that did occur were balanced between the two speakers. But, when women conversed with men, not only did more interruptions occur, 96 percent of them involved men interrupting women.

Based on her doctoral research in sociology at the University of California Pamela Fishmen came to this conclusion: "Both men and women regarded topics introduced by women as tentative whereas topics introduced by the men were treated as topics to be pursued. The women...did much of the necessary work of interaction, starting conversations, and then working to maintain them."

Recall that gender differences are most visible when women and men are in **interaction** not when they are in same sex groups. As Maccoby has shown us, personality tests and other measures of gender differences are not apparent until *women and men are in interaction.*

The differences in female–male perceptions aroused Dr. Antonia Abbey's curiosity (1982). She was with some friends at a bar cordially sharing a table with two male strangers. It seemed to Abbey that the men misinterpreted the women's friendliness as a show of sexual interest—so much so the women "finally had to excuse themselves from the table to avoid an awkward scene" (p. 830).

Abbey wondered if women send out messages they are not aware of and if men read into women's behavior and words meanings that are not there. She paired mixed–sex couples who were instructed to have brief conversations during which they were observed by another mixed–sex pair. Afterwards, each participant reported on what they experienced or observed.

Abbey found men perceive women's friendliness as *sexually provocative*. Women correctly identified other women's *friendliness* for what it was or detected a sexual theme when it was truly present in the mind and behavior of the woman.

The males in the study rated females' behavior as significantly more seductive than females rated females' behavior. Male observers thought the women were attracted and interested in the men—coming on to them— more than the female observers thought they were. Also, the males in the study were significantly more attracted to their female partners than the women were to them.

Abbey's research shows definite differences in the perceptions of men and women; men interpret the friendly posture of women as sexual although the women were not sending a sexual message.

Identity as a Human Being

Abbey's study demonstrates that women and men could get into serious difficulty because of the distinctions in their communication styles. Gilligan's research (1982) describes another communication difference between the sexes.

She asked women in her sample, "How would you describe yourself to yourself?" Women, *in every case*, responded by connecting their identity to being a future mother, present wife, daughter, adopted child, or past lover.

The women in the study were professional women yet none mentioned their academic or professional lives in their description of themselves. Women defined themselves through relationships of intimacy, care, and connection with others.

According to Gilligan, men's and women's *relational* orientations are significantly different as it relates to self-definition:

> Women stay with, build on, and develop in context of attachment and affiliation with others.... Women's sense of self becomes very much organized around being able to make, and then to maintain affiliations and relationships. ...Eventually, for many women, the threat of disruption of an affiliation is something closer to a total loss of self (p. 169).

Brannon's observations dovetail with Gilligan's. Men defined their *identity* through power and separation which they achieved through work. Their sense of self-identity, according to Robert Brannon (1976), falls loosely into five general themes:

1. No Sissy Stuff: Men avoid the stigma of all stereotyped feminine characteristics and qualities, including openness and vulnerability.

2. The Big Wheel: Success, status, and the need to be looked up to.

3. The Sturdy Oak: A manly air of toughness, confidence.

4. Give 'em Hell!: The aura of aggression, violence, and daring.

5. The Sexual Stud (added by Robert Doyle, 1986, p. 90).

Men cannot cross the sexual boundary by wearing anything feminine unless they are willing to pay a heavy social, economic, and psychological price. However, women wear pants and some even considered themselves "tomboys" without harm to their self–image.

Since maleness is of higher status, women can emulate things that are male without being stigmatized. But, the man who decides to dress *down* to a woman's status violates the male code, the social code, and often, the legal code.

We have learned there are differences in personality and role expectations for women and men. A two–step process is in order if we are to make good use of this information:

1. Acknowledge there are differences and that neither sex is "in the right";

2. Work toward change in yourself and with your partner—do not try to bend the other to your will.

The following chapter defines power, identifies who has it and explains the ways in

which power is manifested *inter*personally. You will enhance your loving relationships when you understand how to acquire and use power—appropriately—with the opposite sex.

7

WHO'S GOT THE POWER?

Wives, submit to your own husbands, as onto the Lord. For the husband is the head of the wife, as Christ is the head of the church.

—Ephesians 5:23-24

Should wives submit to their husbands? Would a woman in her right mind choose to be dominated in a relationship? Wouldn't everyone choose equality? Actually, not everyone agrees.

Ephesians dictates, "Women, *submit* to your own husband," whereas women are likely to prefer that men love them with justice. Therefore, if men behaved properly, women's need to submit would be moot. However, men often don't act properly but they still lay claim to dominance.

The woman who submits to male dominance may get lucky and have a husband who respects her rights. If she gets a dominating or uncaring man in the marital draw, life will be difficult for her.

There's an alternative to either the husband or wife being given or taking the power to dominate: **equality**. And even when equality is the goal equality is easier to wish for than to develop in a relationship.

If a woman finds herself in an unequal relationship, she can develop her own power in a variety of ways. Also, men can learn to share power and use it wisely to enhance, not dominate, a relationship. Not all women, however, seek equality.

Phyliss Schlafly (1988) believes motherhood and marriage are natural for women and that male dominance should be happily and dutifully accepted. To Schlafly, dominance—at least in a Christian marriage—is benign. To make her point, she provides a fuller quote from Ephesians [see introdution to this chapter]:

> Husbands, love your wives, even as Christ also loved the church, and gave Himself for it.... Let everyone of you in particular so love his wife even as himself; and the wife see that she reverence her husband.

If husbands loved wives as they love themselves, what harm would flow from that? None, according to Schlafly. "If you complain about servitude to a husband, servitude to a boss will be more intolerable. Everyone in the world has a boss of some kind" (p. 80). The not so hidden assumption in Schlafly's position is that if you are a woman someone will rule you, it's just a question of which male in a woman's life will dominate. Then, isn't the best choice of ruler a husband who also loves you?

A dominant but loving husband may seem benign to someone who'd been trained to be taken care of but all adults should aspire to take care of themselves. If you trust your fate to others, if you approach your life without sufficient power, you are a slave waiting for a master, a victim waiting for a victimizer.

To determine your own life course it is necessary to understand and to develop power. Let's explore the nature of power and how to use it to improve yourself and your relationships.

Power Over: Traditional Power

Power-over is the domination of one person by another. It is the power males use with one another and with women. Traditional power, social power, and physical force are additional forms of domination or power-over.

Traditional power is based upon "what has been" as the basis of what is right and therefore, should be. If a society is traditional, it is patriarchal. In a *patriarchy*, all men have power over all women. There may be exceptions, as when a queen rules or a woman—such as Margaret Thatcher—becomes Prime Minister. Even in these instances the *mechanisms of social control* remain in the hands of men. For example, protocol dictates that the Queen passes her temporary power to a prince, *not to a princess*. With few if any exceptions, laws and religious principles certify the correctness of male domination.

The nation's Roman Catholic Bishops (November 18, 1992) rejected a Pastoral

Letter, favored by the Vatican that would have reinforced the Church's traditional teachings about women. They did this despite the reported stricture from the Vatican that the Bishops not even discuss the ban on women becoming priests.

Custom and tradition arc the primary sources of men's authority over women. Being a man is considered a legitimate reason for exercising power over females. In the Western world, where equality between the sexes is closer to reality than in most places, it still raises fewer eyebrows when a man exerts power over a woman than when a woman bosses a man. When a man takes orders from a woman, it creates definite strains in their relationship and is unusual when it happens.

Granted that pure patriarchy has been significantly modified in urban, industrial America, the deck is still stacked against women in our society. Equality remains more an ideal than a reality. Historically women promised to honor and obey the husband. Some ceremonies continue this tradition of men's domination.

Of coursc, times change and so do gender relations. In April 1990, the Mormons revised their *Endowment* ritual by deleting the pledge of strict wifely obedience to the husband. Women may now pledge obedience to God.

Is the double standard a thing of the past? Consider the reaction to Magic Johnson's revelation that he has HIV (AIDS virus) and that he contracted it from one (or more) of the hundreds of women he has sex with. He's hailed as a courageous hero and served briefly on the President's AIDS Commission. Suppose a well-known female athlete announced that she had contracted the HIV virus by sleeping with hundreds of men. Would she be hailed a hero or labeled a whore and a slut? How likely is it that she would be asked to serve on President's AIDS Commission?

In traditional relationships, women's roles require that they defer to men. In relationships based on equality, friendship and love, there is no need for entrenched, gender based power. Decisions are made by consensus with the full voluntary cooperation of both parties. In both the private and the public sectors, male dominance is more the rule than the exception.

Social Power

In its broadest sense, social power is defined as **the success of one person, group or force to influence how others feel, think or behave.** Social power is the *power-over others.*

One manifestation of social power resides in our private and public educational systems. Traditionally, men have been the developers, holders and dispensers of knowledge and expertise in our society. However, since increasing numbers of women are now in college and graduate schools, we can expect women to become increasingly powerful as they develop their expertise and earn their credentials. Women are more likely to develop themselves fully in all female settings. Why?

In August 1990, the nation's newspapers carried a photo of young women in agony and despair. These were Mills College women grieving and protesting their Board of Trustee's decision to enroll male undergrads for the first time in their 138-year history. Why such agony over gender integration on the campus? These students knew the value of an educational setting without men. They did not want to share their college with men because their very presence changes the atmosphere of learning.

Students at Mount Hollyoke, Smith, Scripps, Wellesley and other women's colleges supported their sisters' protest. They know that when males are present, they become dominant.

Women educated in sex–segregated colleges develop such confidence in themselves that, "out East," men identify them as "Smith" or "Vassar," women. These women are recognized for their confidence, competence and assertiveness. In short, they don't act like *traditional women.* Mills' students didn't want men, with their preordained advantages, to ruin their educational experience.

In 1960 there were 298 women's colleges; now there are 94. Women's power would be enhanced if the trend was reversed.

Gender discrimination is evident long before the college years. One study (using video tape) demonstrated that even when women teachers were told that they were being evaluated for gender partiality in the classroom, they still did such things as briefly compliment the girls on their overall work and spend more time critiquing and correcting the boy's work.

Coercive Force: Violence On The Home Front

In domestic relations *coercive force* is too often used by men to claim *power-over* women. From 1969 to 1989 the percentage of murders of one spouse by the other has declined from 13% of all murders to 6.5%. However, incidents where husbands killed wives increased from 53% to 63% in the same twenty–year period.

We do not have reliable statistics for men's physical violence against their wives but it is estimated that 1.6 million wives are beaten each year. Although wives assault husbands at approximately the same rate they are assaulted by their husbands, women are at greater risk of being injured or killed in these confrontations.

The National Crime Survey (1991) studied 535,000 women from 1979 to 1987. The data revealed that of the 2 million violent crimes against women, 25% were committed by lovers or family members, 27% by others the women knew, and 44% were assaults by strangers. Men had twice as many violent crimes committed against them but only 4% were by family members or lovers and 27% were committed by friends or acquaintances, 69% by strangers. In short, women have more to fear from people they know than from those they don't.

Women are at a serious disadvantage when it comes to safety. If they are raped, they are pilloried again for having been provocative or careless. They are believed to have *gotten what they deserved.* The William Kennedy Smith-Patrcia Bowman rape trial in Florida resulted in his acquittal. Analysts believe Bowman wasn't believed—at least in part—because she was wearing sexy undergarments and went to the Kennedy compound late at night.

Some states have passed laws trying to protect women against being violated a second time by the criminal justice system. Nonetheless, any rape counseling group will tell you the woman who reports a rape is exposed to insensitive medical personnel, police, courts, family, friends, and neighbors. The manner in which a rape victim is handled by the authorities after the rape compounds the damage.

Though outrageous, it is common for the police and the courts to act only after numerous assaults result in injury or death. Attempts have been made in some cities to prevent repeated domestic violence against women by passing laws that allow police to arrest the alleged perpetrator without them having seen the actual assault. This reduces but does not eliminate repeated violence in a family. Here are a few examples of women's vulnerability.

In Troy, Michigan, a husband hid in the shadows at the roadside near his house and shot his wife to death with a high caliber pistol as she left for work (1989). On several occasions her attorney had brought motions before the court to have him removed from the home because of his violence and threats. The judge ruled to preserve the husband's rights to stay in the home until the divorce became final.

In Michigan (1991) a husband was sentenced to five to fifteen years for raping and beating his wife. This was but one of repeated assaults resulting in humiliation and injury. While in jail awaiting trial, the husband tried to arrange for his wife's beating and disfigurement. Unfortunately for him, he was soliciting this service from an undercover policeman. He'll be tried on this charge later. The wife is sure that he'll make a "b-line" to kill her when he gets out of prison.

One western Michigan community has a policy requiring women to wait three days after a domestic assault before police take the complaint. Many women have been harmed during the required wait.

Women are caught in a deadly double bind. If they seek legal protection from their assailants, they are still not protected. The assaulter often becomes enraged by her complaint and harms her again. If women stay in the violent relationship, they are regarded as partially to blame.

If women counter-assault or kill the tormentor—either during or after an attack—they are likely to be convicted of assault or murder. A few states, like Ohio, are now recognizing the vulnerability of women and why they killed their attackers. These women are being selectively released from prison.

Coercion and Power: Always Wrong?

Serious problems arise when too much power resides with one partner. Significant differences in power always reduces intimacy. Consider this example:

> When Kim, 37, and Jon, 49, came to us for counseling, Kim was obviously anxious. She spoke quickly, "Is there a way to eliminate a person's anger?" Our question to Kim was: "Are you the angry person, and if so, do you want to eliminate your anger?"
>
> Kim replied, "I get angry in response to my husband's anger. I try to stay calm so I don't rile him but he keeps pushing me until I can't control myself." Kim went on to say that her husband was regarded as mild mannered by his dental patients. However, at home he was "belligerent and confrontational" and on several occasions slapped her.
>
> Jon stared at Kim as though she was speaking Chinese and he was Russian. He flatly denied slapping her, jumped out of his chair and said he would not subject himself to her lies.
>
> Kim continued the therapy session that night; Jon did not return. After two years of therapy, Kim was able to resolve her anxieties and learned to take care of herself physically and psychologically.
>
> During her recovery, she was advised to leave the house if there was any threat of physical abuse or if she felt frightened. Under no circumstances should one "tough it out" when there are physical threats or violence.

We strongly caution women to avoid being the victims in *power-over* arrangements. Men are raised in a world in which competition is noble, and conflict—even violence—is seen as a necessary tool to reach their goals. Some men take it as their birthright to use force to get their way. Often, violence is excused by blaming the victim: "She just kept after me until I couldn't stand it, so I cuffed her. She brought it on herself. I'm sorry I hit her but she needs to learn not to press me beyond my endurance." So said Andrew.

In one of his rages, Andrew, 34, threw Barb, 29, against the refrigerator. He had slapped and pushed her before but never with such violence. He was having increasing difficulties with his sexual performance and he blamed her. This time she was truly frightened and gathered her two children and a few belongings, hustled them into the van and sped off to her mother's house. Her family suggested she needed counseling to understand herself and her husband.

Andrew is a semi-skilled worker who feels he should have gone further in life; he feels inferior and uses alcohol to make life more bearable. Recently, he's added violence to his verbal abuse. When Barb left, he started looking for her. He called her friends and finally found her at her mother's.

He begged her to return. He explained the stress he'd been under and protested, "It wasn't really me that hit you; it was someone I don't want to be and won't ever be again." This confused Barb. She wanted to believe him, yet she knew he was becoming increasingly abusive.

Barb called to describe the situation. We agreed it would be wise for her to stay out of the home at least until he'd been in therapy and brought his violence under control. She thought the better course of action would be to divorce him. Their life as a couple had become unsatisfactory over the years. She now made more money than he did and could no longer bear the threat of violence.

Unwisely, but not without precedent, Barb eventually decided to return to the home and give him "one more chance." Eight months later we received another call from her: Life was unbearable and she needed help to leave the marriage.

Barb is likely to be judged harshly by others for her failure to end the relationship earlier. This is especially true because she has a good job and can support herself.

What should women like Barb do to improve their life? Should they seek—as Schlafly recommends—a dominant but more "just" husband, a more benevolent dictator? Or, should women avoid situations in which someone can exercise power-over them? If women want egalitarian relationships, they will have to develop their personal power, their *power-to*.

Personal Power or Power-To

Personal power or *power-to*, is based on the ability to control one's own fate and to use one's personal resources to influence others' behaviors, thoughts and feelings. It is also used to **prevent** others from using their power over you. This is also called, "countervailing power."

Personal power consists of ability and skills developed through self-discipline (Marilyn French, 1985, p. 504). Personal power exists independently of money, position or other trappings associated with high status.

When personal power is operating, people will cooperate willingly, even enthusiastically. The possessor of personal power may be charismatic, able to lead by the sheer force of their personality. The charismatic person uses power to influence, to heal, to control, or to capture the popular imagination. (Charisma can also be applied negatively.)

What if you aren't one of the chosen few who can use personal, charismatic power to get what you want? Then it becomes doubly important to understand what power is, how to acquire it and then to use it in appropriate ways. There are other mechanisms of power.

Persuasion as Power

Through *persuasion,* an eloquent, verbally skilled person can cause others to think, feel or act in desired ways. Compliance can occur at a very subtle level with the application of power so gentle that the influenced person is unaware of the means by which they've been changed.

For example, those attending real estate seminars are hyped-up by the promoters to buy expensive materials and leave the seminar excited and full of enthusiasm. The real lesson they learn about property is that their own assets have been shifted to someone else—the seminar organizers—through persuasion.

Argument refers to a discussion based on a disagreement, dispute or debate. It is a contest in which the goal is to forcefully persuade the other. Women and men have distinct styles when they argue. This was true for Ken and Amanda.

In a therapy session we listened to them talk about their lives and we were struck by how much Ken talked and how little Amanda contributed. Several times we turned to Amanda to ask about her version of what Ken presented as her thoughts and feelings only to have Ken interrupt. When directly asked to talk about her views, Amanda demurred with the explanation, "Ken knows how I feel and he's a better talker." Amanda deliberately gave Ken her power. Why?

Amanda had been worn down by Ken's persuasive style. Like a salesman, Ken was able to convince Amanda he was the person in the relationship who understood people and situations. Therefore, it wasn't necessary for her to have opinions or to express them. If she did, he criticized or out-talked her.

Persuasive power can be helpful or hurtful in creating intimacy in relationships. Sexual power also can move people apart or bring them closer together.

Sex and Power

Sexual "rewarding" is most often practiced by women. They offer themselves to men in ways that please or satisfy men's needs. Since sex is a recurrent desire it can be a significant source of power in relationships either as a reward or punishment. A straight forward use of sex for power occurs when a woman says to her boy friend, "Why should I have sex with you when you don't love me enough to marry me?"

There are more subtle uses of sex as power, as in the case of a middle–class couple, Alma and Grant.

Alma, 42, is a homemaker. Her husband, Grant, 44, is a professional who makes a good living and inherited money from his father. He is ill-disposed to spend much of it on Alma but is generous with himself. This creates significant conflicts between them because Alma tries to keep up with their wealthy friends by the way she furnishes and runs the house and keeps herself.

Grant always takes her requests for money under advisement, never giving it to her when she asks for it. Eventually, Alma realized if she asked Grant for money when he was sexually aroused but before he was satisfied, her wishes were "granted."

Grant is as greedy about sex as he is about his other pleasures which he's willing to pay for. He realized that giving Alma permission to acquire what she wants makes her favorably disposed toward him. Under these circumstances, both of them enjoyed love making. But, when he refuses her requests, she's angry and disappointed and avoids arousing him or responding to his overtures. "How can I think about sex when I'm so disturbed," she's says.

Alma never offers to *trade* sex for things she wants but Grant understands if she is upset about anything he's done or won't do, there will be no love making.

Alma and Grant's pattern of using sex and money as reward and punishment, as power chips in their relationship, is relatively obvious. Often, the use of sex in power games can be subtle and difficult to detect. This was the case with Carey and Frank.

Carey works part-time. Frank, an executive with a national corporation, is overweight and has high blood pressure. In their late forties, Carey and Frank live with their two teenagers. As the children have become busier with friends and interests outside the home, Carey and Frank have more exposure so each other. As a result of their newly found time together, their relationship and sexual problems have increased in intensity.

Relationship problems aren't new for this couple. They have not communicated well either verbally or physically during most of their marriage. Neither of them has a particularly strong sex drive. A forceful person at work, Frank expects to be obeyed at home. When Carey resists Frank's will, or is ignorant of what he expects, Frank withdraws. Nothing she did or said hastened the restoration of their relationship. Therefore, she learned to *wait-him-out*. Carey knew Frank would eventually want to have sex. When he made his move it provided them with an opportunity to settle their argument.

With the kids taking less of her time, Carey decided to put her education to use and developed a small business. At the same time she was less concerned with Frank's demands. He reacted with hurt and withdrew even more.

When Carey's business reached a stage that did not require her constant attention, she realized she was witnessing the slow dissolution of her marriage. She was determined to improve it. Since sex had occasionally been a useful way to get close to Frank in the past, she decided to be more loving with him. At this point complications set in.

Frank's high blood pressure now had to be controlled by drugs. A side effect of one of the drugs made it difficult for him to maintain an erection. Frank reacted by avoiding sex with his wife. However, he compensated with increased sexual banter at social gatherings. When Carey made efforts to arouse him at home, he withdrew. If he thought Carey might want sex, he'd start an argument to mask his impotence.

Carey encouraged him to see his physician and accompanied him. The doctor suggested a change in medication and Frank said he'd consider it. Nothing changed. Frank refused to use new medication with the excuse that he did not want to chance the effects of some new drug.

Withholding sex was Frank's way of punishing Carey for her independence. It was difficult for Frank to admit this to himself but once this dynamic was uncovered in therapy and the couple found new ways to communicate, they were eventually able to solve their sexual problem.

Betty's experience with sex and power helps us understand just how complex sex-power dynamics can get.

Betty reported she had two major problems when she was in high school: She was rejected by her high school's cliques; and her mother gave her mixed messages about men and sex. Her mother encouraged her to date when she was thirteen and Betty complied to please her mother.

Betty's mother took great pride in the way her little girl looked and encouraged her to dress in provocative outfits. Betty was required to give her mother a blow by blow account of the evening before she could go to bed. More confusing to Betty was the fact that no boy she went out with met her mother's approval.

Betty had so little power in her life she began to take what she now considers to be a "strange delight": She would arouse her dates, submit to sex, but she herself *felt* nothing. To Betty, feeling nothing was power. In her

own way she'd found a way to be free of domination by
others.

Other Subtle Forms Of Power

Women often use subtle power approaches
that include persuasion, suggestion and
manipulation. Some subtle approaches are
consciously designed and some unconsciously
motivated. For example, Valery's approach
involved a conscious effort to increase her
power in Mel's life.

Valery, at thirty-two, was a veteran of many
unhappy relationships. Her misfortunes with men had
sapped her self-confidence and increased her sense of
desperation. Mel was her occasional lover. When he
couldn't find anyone more to his liking or he was in
between women, he called on Valery.

Valery was an adopted child whose adoptive parents
saw her more as a cog in their machinery than a human
being in her own right. This made her a push over for
Mel's style.

She could tell when Mel was going to dump her; he
made no secret of it. He would announce, "I've found
another woman." To preserve her place in his life, she
dropped by his apartment, commented on how untidy the
place was and offered to clean it. She would take off
work, clean his apartment and do his clothes. She also
bought groceries for his pantry and brought food she'd
cooked for him on the pretense the meals were "left-
overs."

When he had trouble with a girlfriend, Valery acted
interested and listened to his troubles—all the while
hoping he'd leave the woman. She would offer him
helpful suggestions about how women operated hoping

he would appreciate her and hasten the end to his relationship.

Often, after these "listening sessions," she had to stop her car on the way home and vomit. Valery never let him know how much his thoughtlessness hurt her. She did anything she could think of to keep in his favor and hurry his latest romance to its end.

Whereas Valery was desperate and paid a heavy price for her attempt to gain power with Mel, Joyce was more subtle in her dealings with her husband, Howard.

Joyce discovered early in her seventeen year marriage that she had to "beat around the bush" with Howard. This meant Joyce could never be direct and tell Howard exactly what she wanted or what she thought. When she made a direct request he found some excuse or mechanism to frustrate her and to deny her wishes.

To gain more power, she used various indirect but effective approaches. "For example," she said, "our house is totally my doing. Howard did not want to move; he did not think HE could afford it. Damn him. I work and bring in money too.

"So I started a campaign by telling him how 'real estate values are always moving up,' and how 'land is the best investment,' and that 'the neighborhood we're in is deteriorating.' I slipped this garbage into our conversations on a regular basis until he began to spout exactly the same words. In the meantime, I spent hours looking at property and houses on my way to and from work.

"We now have a beautiful house. I built it. I found the land, bought it, hired the contractor and the architect. I saw the whole thing through. I tried to get Howard to make decisions about the interior but he caught on to the fact that he'd be deferring to my wishes so he'd have nothing to do with it. Now he collars anyone who will listen and tells them how clever he was to build when the market was low.

"I'm sick of having to manage the marriage and my husband. I want an equal relationship. Howard thinks he is the king and controls his castle. What he doesn't understand is that I handle everything and make all decisions. He goes to work, comes home and talks like a big shot. I feel like stuffing his mouth with his socks when he starts describing how clever he's been.

"I never get credit. I do get what I want but it's like living a secret, inner life."

Although Joyce's method of power is subtle, her dissatisfaction is reaching its limit. We doubt that Joyce's emotions will remain contained. She appears ready to release her undercover style and shift into a direct approach, one that will be healthy for Joyce but may be the beginning of the end of the relationship.

Weakness As Power

The idea that there is power in weakness seems to be an oxymoron (where opposite or contradictory terms are combined). In reality, presenting yourself as the weak, deficient, needy person can be powerful because there is an ethic in our society that instructs us to be kind to those who are in trouble or who are inferior. Another societal norm gives "sickness" a special status: As long as the sick person plays the sick role correctly, he or she is relieved of most obligations—except to do everything they can to get well.

Men, in particular, have been trained to come to the aid of the "damsel in distress." Women understand this consciously as well as intuitively and they often use it in relationships. No? Think of how many times you have asked others to help you when you were perfectly capable of doing it yourself. Have you ever deliberately presented yourself to a male as helpless or in need of help to attract him?

In short, the "weaker" person may prevail in a power struggle. We learn to do this as children and carry it on into adulthood. Consider how *weakness* served Ray's purposes.

After their second child was born Ray's wife, Brenda, returned to work as an executive secretary. Her $40,000 salary and bonuses were enough to satisfy her needs and those of the children so she decided she no longer had to tolerate Ray's combination of infidelity and nastiness.

The divorce papers came as a shock to Ray. Brenda could not be dissuaded but Ray was so distraught his ulcers flared-up and he had to be hospitalized and have part of his stomach removed. When he begged and pleaded for just a little support in his hour of need, Brenda felt a sense of power that she'd never had before and suspended the divorce action. She did not want to appear to be heartless.

She felt she had to care for him for the children's sake, and she enjoyed his groveling. Ray's convalescence was protracted and he lost his job as a lighting and fixture salesman during his recuperation. He made himself useful around the house, kept things clean and saw to the needs of the children.

Weeks grew into months and melted into fourteen years. Ray voluntarily and permanently assumed the role

of *househusband*. When their youngest child left the
home for the military, Brenda re-evaluated her situation,
sought counseling, and came to realize Ray had his way
by becoming weak. She started a new divorce action.
Ray tried many new "take care of me" routines, but to no
avail. Ray went to live with his elderly mother after the
divorce and kept house for her.

Crying, breaking down, or humbling one's
self are just some of the ways that people gain
power from weakness. There are few among us
who have never feigned an illness or developed
symptoms to get our way with parents,
teachers, spouses, or employers.

Women easily fall prey to this kind of
weakness maneuver because they have been
trained to be caretakers. Time and again we
see female clients who are basically through
with their marriage but cannot make the final
break because they are afraid of the pain it will
cause their husbands and family.

The societal myth that men are more
competent than women is used by some
women to their supposed advantage. Viewed as
the "weaker sex," women get men to do many
things for them by presenting themselves as
incompetent. Pomazal and Clore (1973), and
West (1975), found that men were likelier to
assist a helpless female than a helpless male
(Doyle, 1985).

What's the harm in using weakness for
advantage? The person using this technique
loses self esteem. It also sets up a dependency
upon the other party. After years of relying
upon others, what happens when life makes

demands and others are not available to meet them?

To illustrate, when a mother has traded on her helplessness in the marriage and the husband dies, she may expect the children to fill his role. Many husbands are in the same fix. Having left the cooking, cleaning, and social arrangements to their wives, the widower hasn't the slightest idea of how to prepare healthy meals or to maintain social relationships. His life is shortened because of poor nutrition. Social relationships are also important to health and longevity. Without a wife, if his social life withers so does he.

A person may also feel weak and powerless when withholding is used in the power game.

Withholding

Withholding can be a powerful punishment mechanism. *Punishment power* ranges from physical assault and murder to showing displeasure. We've all experienced the power of withholding such as the "silent treatment."

The silent treatment is used by one person or group to bring another into line. Among the Amish, *shunning* an offender consists of the community refusing to speak or to otherwise interact with the offending person. The power in the method is that the person is treated as if she/he does not exist. Since the Amish community is self-contained and there are no others with whom to interact, you can imagine the price this punishment extracts.

There is a parallel to shunning in family relationships in that one's family is generally the source of fundamental acceptance. If someone in the family refuses to acknowledge someone else, they are isolated and thereby punished.

Autonomy and Power

Autonomy and power are separate but related experiences. *Power* refers to the capacity of one person to influence another in a desired direction irrespective of the other's will. *Autonomy* is defined as being able to function independently.

To the extent that you are politically, socially, economically and psychologically independent of your spouse, you have power to *be yourself* in the relationship. Nevertheless, there are economically self-sufficient women and men who are so *psychologically* tied to each other they lose their self-determination.

Often, women who are able to provide for themselves stay in and foster bad relationships because they cannot bring themselves to take their share of power. Though they allow men to dictate to them, they complain loudly about their fate.

No one is completely within the power of another nor is he/she incapable of resisting the will of others. Camus (1969) argued that everyone has the capacity to say "NO, this far, no farther!" Even the dictator or slave master is powerless when the other declares this ultimate "no." The AmerIndians couldn't be enslaved by the colonists because they preferred death to servitude.

Autonomy is a matter of degree. If you do not understand how *independent* you can be and how *inter*dependent you need to be for your own good, you lose personal and social power.

Power has many forms. It can be gained from many sources including higher status family members.

Derivative Power

Women who live in the shadow of their husbands are seldom viewed as autonomous because so much of their lives are spent in the service of others. When Barbara Bush, the President's wife, was invited to be the commencement speaker at Wellesley College in 1990, all hell broke loose. One hundred fifty Wellesley women signed a petition declaring that Barbara Bush was an unsuitable choice because her status came not from her own efforts but from her husband's prominence.

Mrs. Bush became a political wife in an era when it was expected that all women would subordinate their interests to those of their husbands. Barbara Bush has accomplishments of her own but they've been dwarfed by her husband's status.

Similarly, Marilyn Quayle, the Vice President's wife, came under the scrutiny of The Washington Post (1992) which

characterized her as potentially "the most
influential first lady in American history" if her
husband, Dan, becomes president. The
impression left with the reader is that she
would become too powerful in the affairs of
state because she is the power behind the
throne.

Paula Blanchard, the ex-spouse of the
Governor of Michigan, referred to advantages
that come from another person's wealth,
position or influence as *derivative power*
(Blanchard, 1990). According to her, "It
usually comes from men because men still hold
most of the economic, political and social
power." She does not apologize for the source
of her power: "If it's derivative power rather
than original power, so be it. Women have to
stop being such purists about power. We must
grab power wherever we can find it and put it
to work for us and our causes" (p. 58).

Mentoring, another form of derivative
power, is a practice wherein a person in
authority is helpful to someone coming up
through the system. The mentor is more than
a superior; she/he is a guide and advocate. It's
a common experience for men but less often
for women, to move rapidly up in the
corporate world with the aid of a mentor.

Sometimes, men mentor women as Jack
mentored Amy.

Amy, 28, and Jack, 31, met when they worked as
engineers in the same firm. When she joined the
company, Jack, handsome and athletically built, was
Amy's supervisor. He liked her personally and
professionally and soon became her mentor. A few

months into their professional relationship, they became romantically involved.

Amy didn't stay Jack's subordinate for long. With Jack's help and her own talent Amy gained confidence, recognition and promotions. Soon, she was promoted to Jack's level.

As sometimes happens with a mentor, Jack felt betrayed and unappreciated. Their love relationship complicated things and he became competitive and jealous. He acted like a bully. When they argued, Jack would put on a threatening anger display. He ranted and raved and refused to listen to her arguments.

The next day he would be at her door with apologies. Actually, in his mind, he felt justified in his anger. He wanted the relationship but he could not tolerate the equality Amy demanded. Both of them wanted their relationship to continue so they agreed to try therapy.

His main complaint was, "She makes me feel that I am number 10 on her list; everyone else, including her co-workers and friends, come first. I don't like the way I act but I can't stop or change it. She does things that make me crazy."

Amy saw it differently: "Yes, I do things that make him crazy—like talking to a co-worker. I think he's out of line and that he wants me to walk in his shadow. The truth is, I put Jack first. I'm always available to him but I'm tired of worrying about what he will think if he sees me talking to someone or how he'll react if my phone rings when he's with me. Frankly, I think he has a problem. He has to be totally in control and feel like *macho man* or life is hell."

They tried to work their differences out in therapy. Meanwhile, they continued their pattern of breaking up then making up. Eventually, Amy decided to end the relationship saying she "couldn't take it anymore."

Jack came in one last time to say he had done everything humanly possible to please Amy. He sought the therapist's support hoping to vindicate himself and to leave therapy having the last word.

We hope that Amy continued her career climb. We know it is difficult for women to reach the highest levels of self-actualization because there's the suspicion that without using the coattails of the powerful male, there would have been no success. Amy's fate is similar to that of minority members who, because they use government programs to overcome the results of past discrimination, are not fully valued by others. It's one of the Catch 22s in life: Without an opportunity, no one can prove their merit; with a forced opportunity, no one can be sure of their merit.

The Overall Picture: Understanding And Using Power In Your Life

Power is an ingredient in every relationship; understanding the role of power in relationships is vital to their success. To be in control of your own fate—to the extent that is possible—it is necessary to have ample personal and social power. It is also necessary to set realistic goals that allow for the differences between men and women. Power should be used constructively in relationships.

Day to day power resides in inner feelings of strength, the ability to determine your own stance and to stick to it. When problems arise because of power differentials in relationships, there are ways to resolve them.

1. **Bring up the problem and focus only on that problem.** It is necessary to separate the real issues from those that are insignificant. For example, you may appreciate your husband's status and income but become angry because he is inconsiderate about calling when he is late. Present your position to him in a business–like manner, not when you are at the height of your anger or deep in your hurt.

An angry presentation will be another blurring factor; the other party will defend themselves rather than listen to the issue. He may say, "You don't understand, my business requires flexibility." Or, "There wasn't a phone handy and you're always bitching no matter what I do."

2. **Select an issue and focus on it, *exclusively*.** In the example above, the problem is the husband does not call when he's going to be late. Naturally, your feelings are hurt and you feel he does not respect you and your interests. You may feel he has time for others but doesn't care about you or the children.

Stay with the issue; do not add other problems. If he refuses to stick to the "calling when he's late topic," be patient. Stay centered. If the matter isn't resolved right then, no problem. Relax, and choose another time to discuss it. But, continue your efforts.

After an argument, there may be a temporary change in the behavior. This is no substitute for a *resolution*. If there isn't an agreed upon understanding and solution, the problem will probably surface again.

By clarifying an issue and staying with it until there's a resolution you gain personal power. Power, as we have seen, comes from a variety of sources.

The the next chapter, finances and money, demonstrates how one's monetary assets can be positive forces in a relationship or be used to control and manipulate others.

FINANCES

Money is power.

—Just About Everyone

Resource power

What are *resources* and why are they so important in gender relations? Webster's Dictionary defines resource as something that lies ready for use or can be drawn upon for aid or to take care of need; available money or property; wealth; assets. In social life, resources translate into power.

Do you have resource power? To find out, ask yourself some simple questions.

1. Do you have, apart from anyone else in the family, money, property, wealth, or other assets?

2. Can you use your assets or dispose of them as you please?

3. Do you have access to these resources at a moment's notice?

4. Do you have an occupation or other way to add to your resources if you so desire or must you depend upon others?

Why are resources critical? Because, resources are one key to power. To illustrate: "Why didn't you leave him if he beats you?" we've asked the battered wife. Masochism (the need for abuse) may explain some abusive relationships but we usually find, as in Madeline's case, that alternatives were limited because she had no resources of her own.

Madeline, 30, has two children and has been married to Dave, 36, for twelve years. When she complained about his boozing and absence from home, he kneed her in the stomach several times for "bitching." You may ask, "why does she tolerate such brutality?" She had no rational answer.

Friends and sibs who saw how Dave treated her took her aside and warned her about being so dependent upon him. She didn't seem to understand what they were saying.

At times she made token moves to generate more power by looking into college programs. When she raised the subject of starting college, Dave was dead set against it. That ended her college plans despite the fact that she knew education could lead to independence.

Before coming to therapy she consulted an attorney about divorce. She intended to pressure Dave, not divorce him. She wanted a new car and he wouldn't consider it. But, he was impressed enough by her resort to legal action that he bought her a "previously owned" automobile.

Madeline gave up the idea of attending college. Instead, she reverted to manipulation—a time-worn technique of the powerless. Madeline wheedled what she could out of Dave and cemented her inferior position.

Whereas women often seek to acquire resources through their marriage, many men remain in marriages because divorce requires a division of assets. The loss of *their* assets, present and future, is sometimes enough to dissuade men from divorce. We worked with a couple that had tried counseling several times. Joe would agree to counseling and then quit. He couldn't abide Joan but neither could he face the destruction of *his* business.

Joe, 49, a graphic arts specialist, wanted to leave his wife of 27 years, Tess, 50, but after filing for divorce he discovered it was necessary to give an accounting of his assets. Joe refused to disclose his wealth because, he said, "My stuff is mine!" Joe couldn't bear to lose control of the material wealth he'd accumulated.

Joe agreed to counseling on the condition his wife instruct her attorney to withdraw the interrogatory (a legal requirement that he list his assets and liabilities). Tess, eager to preserve the marriage, put the legal proceedings on hold when he promised their life together would improve.

When it became apparent to us Joe was using marriage counseling to manipulate his wife and hang onto his resources, we ended therapy. Tess was willing to tolerate the marriage for a similar reasons: she did not want to give up her life style.

Joe and Tess were reluctant to leave the marriage because they would both suffer economically. This went against their stated values: that people love one another for themselves, not for money and comfort.

Resources are not an open topic of discussion during the courtship. Nevertheless, women, in particular, are given to consider their future spouse's earning power because it will usually determine their life style.

The Importance of Resources

Some people prefer to argue that in a *real relationship* everything is shared or jointly owned. Therefore, it isn't necessary to have independent resources. If this is your thinking then you'd better pray you have a *real relationship.* If you don't, you may be in the same sad shape as millions of widowed, deserted, or divorced people.

In the *real* world—the one of divorce courts—property settlements are often more difficult to resolve than custody issues. Mothers usually get custody of the children but not enough child and spousal support to continue to rear the children in their former lifestyle. Statistics show that after divorce men's standard of living goes up (about 40%) while women's and children's take a dive (about 70%).

A woman with her own resources can leave a terrible situation, if necessary. She's less likely to be seduced or manipulated into tolerating the intolerable if she has her own assets. For one thing, the other person can't feel, "I gotcha" knowing that you can't get along without their support.

We don't advocate the misuse of power but we do emphasize that if you have asset power, you will be taken more seriously. You will not be as vulnerable to the whims or predations of others when you can care for yourself. Too few women are sensitive to resource power since they are "programmed" to be financially cared for by a man. This expectation of being taken care of leads to power deflation. It even affects women who have decent jobs.

Candy, 33, holds a management position with a national mortgage firm; her husband Stuart, 37, is a certified public accountant. Candy complains that Stuart isn't working hard enough to bring in his share of needed family income; Stuart complains Candy is distant and uninterested in sex. They both agree the marriage is in deep trouble.

In our interview with Candy, we helped her understand remote but important forces at work in her life. We pointed out she is working harder and making more of a contribution than Stuart and this runs counter to her programming as a woman.

Candy exploded, "It makes me angry. My father encouraged me to become a business woman. He used to study with me, taught me about the Stock Market and real estate. I was good at math and other business subjects in college. I always wanted to work and was happy in my job until recently...."

She seemed to reflect on what she'd just said. "I just thought of something that hadn't crossed my mind in years. When I first graduated from college, I thought, now it's time to get married and have children. I wasn't going with anyone at the time. Even though my goal seemed to be 'successful business woman,' I guess I drifted into the job market because it was expected of me since that was what I had prepared myself for."

Upon further reflection Candy realized that while she wanted to work, she didn't want to *have* to work. She was getting "burned out" after many years of high output on the job. She still wanted to work but now she wanted to cut down on her hours and responsibilities so she could be home with the kids.

Once Candy realized that an important source of her tension was due to her socialization as a woman, she was able to see why she was angry and dissatisfied. She and Stuart were able to discuss their separate but related needs as individuals and as members of distinct genders. Neither was "to blame"; they were acting our their roles as a woman and man in our society and gendering got them in trouble.

The couple agreed to sell their expensive home and buy one that allowed them to have a decent life style. Candy took a job that permitted time for herself and the children. Stuart increased his workload enough to bring in the extra income they needed to maintain an agreeable level of living.

Money is the Root of All...

Some of Stuart and Candy's problems were grounded in finances. How important is money and assets in a couple's lives?

Blood and Wolfe (1960) studied the effect of resources on power and its relationship to marriage. What they found was not surprising: Resources create power. The power goes to the person who is employed, brings in money, has the education and occupational training, and who is older and has worldly knowledge. (Other factors such as which spouse had family nearby, the socio-economic status of the family they grew up in, personality, intelligence, etc., are also important.)

Blood and Wolfe tested the effect of resources on each partners' decision making and found that 72 percent of couples were relatively equal in making decisions. But, when there were inequalities, husbands dominated eight times more than wives.

Bear in mind this was only one study and it had some flaws. Other studies found American marriages to be much less egalitarian than did Blood and Wolfe.

An important question to be asked and answered is, "Which gender in our society controls the economy?" True, some women are wealthy, but with few exceptions it is money inherited or gained from their relationships with men. Our contention is that whether we look at the national, local or family level, men have traditionally been in control of the economy. That is not to say that women do not make substantial contributions—a second income is increasingly necessary to achieve a decent standard of living.

Men have consolidated their grip on the economy to such an extent that only if they consent can women gain an economic foothold in any significant way. For example, in 1983 Ann Hopkins was refused a partnership by her accounting firm although she brought in more business than any of the other 87 Associates in the corporation. The problem she ran into was that management took exception to her "unfeminine behavior."

She allegedly smoked, cursed, drank beer, did not carry a purse, did not walk or talk *like a woman*, and did not use make-up. In 1990, the courts not only found against the firm's decision to deny Hopkins promotion to Associate, it took the unusual step of redressing this wrong by ordering that she be made a Partner.

A 1990 study (The Detroit News and Free Press, June 24) of the sexual make-up of Michigan's 32 largest public corporations revealed that 25 had no female board members. Less than 6 percent of 573 board seats in the state's 50 largest companies were held by women. No matter which way you cut it, men control the economy.

At the personal level, when a wife's income exceeds her husband's, a man loses one of his usual trump cards in the power game.

> Janice was accepted as a candidate for trainee as an insurance agent. This company interviews the potential agent's spouse as a qualification for employment. When the manager interviewed Janice's husband, he was asked if he would be disturbed if his wife's income was greater than his. Why pose the question? Because, it is still true that marital disharmony is created when women are more successful than their husbands. The company did not want to train an agent who might quit because the husband reacted to being outdone.

To lose financial power violates a man's culturally specified entitlement to dominance over women (Scanzoni and Scanzoni, 1976). If one cannot provide for one's own food, shelter, clothing and other vital goods and services (for example, health care) one does not have *basic economic power*. This puts women in the uncomfortable and potentially devastating position of have to accommodate to intolerable relationships. Without economic power, she is in a poor position to negotiate a better relationship.

Marriage and Money

Money is the highest value in American society so it is bound to be important in relationships. Few people admit to themselves or others that they marry for money. Money considerations are seldom mentioned because that violates the notion marriage is based on love. Nevertheless, money is a factor in the selection of mates and in the power politics of relationships.

The person short on money is likely to be short on power. If you find yourself on the short end of the money–power equation, what can you do? Lisa had this problem.

Lisa, 34, dreaded shopping for the family because Hal, 34, a builder, exerted his control over their relationship by criticizing her purchases and varying the amounts of money he gave her. Every trip to the grocery store was torture because he flew into a rage if she spent too much.

To reduce her stress and to supplement the money he gave her, she began working part time in a card shop. This enabled her to buy some of the things she wanted without running into opposition from Hal. She set her hours so that she was at home when Hal left for work in the morning and back before he returned in the evening. Lisa's strategy worked until Hal realized this weakened his control. He then gave her even less money so she was even more dependent.

Lisa and Hal's money arrangement is an obvious manipulation of money for power. Hal had more money, therefore more power. It was that simple.

Rhonda and Phil illustrate how complicated the money-power formula can become. This couple is in their forties and have three children.

Phil, 40, is an attorney who never completely separated from his mother. Lisa, 39, was trained as a nurse but never held a full time position. Lisa was accustomed to the homemaker role and felt it was important for the kids to have her at home. She wanted to help in the law practice for a time but Phil's mother already worked there.

Phil sought to exert the power at home he never mustered as a child. He would ask Rhonda and the children to choose a vacation place, then veto or change plans in subtle but important ways. When they complained, he invoked his breadwinner role and therefore, his power to spend it carefully.

These maneuvers made Phil less attractive to Rhonda so she rarely agreed to have sex with him. She could not contest his ability to control the events of their lives because he alone knew how much money they really had. Instead, she started her own small business, an art exchange, where people could trade or sell their paintings and sculptures.

From her vantage point as a business woman, Rhonda came across objects that she wanted for her own home. As a power ploy, she signed contracts to purchase art objects and had the bills sent to Phil. Phil, wanting to restore his sex life and to avoid lawsuits for failure to live up to a contract, paid for the objects even though he found them to be ugly and expensive.

Unraveling Rhonda and Phil's intricate money-power tactics was complicated. Money is a difficult subject for couples to discuss in a reasonable way.

In fact, marriages typically begin with little dialogue about how the couple will deal with their finances. Each partner has hidden assumptions about how to deal with money, both assuming that somehow "it will work out." People entering second or subsequent marriages usually come to agreements about money and assets because they realize how divisive these matters are, just as Don and Alice did.

Alice and Don, both professionals and each with three children, decided to get married. They decided to split the household expenses 50-50. Alice makes more money than Don but he's capable of meeting his share of their expenses. Once their mutual expenses are paid, Don and Alice each determine how to allocate the rest of their money. If Alice decides to pay for her children's college education that is up to her. When Don gave his daughter $5,000 toward her wedding expenses that was his decision. They have drawn up their wills to reflect this style of money management. Money is not used for power in their relationship; it is allocated to enhance their relationship.

If you are planning to have children, follow the lead of another couple we've worked with.

They saved before the children came. Part of the wife's savings went into her own account. A legal agreement was drawn up making her sole proprietor of this account. As long as she stayed home to raise the children, a specified portion of his income went into her account.

This couple shows no sign of being in any marital difficulty but if it happened, she would not be destitute. This arrangement reflects a respect on the husband's part for his wife's work in the home and it empowers her with money and trust.

If you don't have your own resources and undergo a divorce, prepare for "Catch 22." If you cannot pay the attorney's retainer and fees you may end up with inexpensive, frustrating, and ineffective legal representation. Generally, you can't even hire an attorney on the promise you'll pay with the settlement you get. There are rules which state divorces cannot be financed on a contingency basis.

Women sometimes think that since their husbands have money their attorney fees will be covered and they can punish their spouses by running up the bill. In many states, the spouse is obligated to pay only a small portion of attorney fees. Women usually find they have to pay their attorney fees out of the settlement.

What To Do About Resources and Money

Women have a tendency to trade their selfhood and freedom for support. In some relationships this works out satisfactorily. But, this kind of arrangement is highly risky for a dependent person. Unemployment, illness, death, desertion, or divorce may enter the picture and create severe difficulties for the person who is not self-supporting. What can you do about this?

1. Before marriage and certainly before having children, live alone and complete your educational and occupational training. If that isn't or wasn't possible, begin a training program for yourself, one class at a time, as soon as you can. Once you are educated or trained, you know you and your children can survive and will not be financially trapped in a marriage.

2. If you have an income of your own, maintain control of it. Be sure you have a bank account and other assets in your name only. There are excellent reasons for having emergency funds: Critical medical treatment, sudden car and home repairs, other crises, and for just plain peace of mind. Your mate may take a dim view of your having separate assets. Be prepared for: "Don't you love me? Don't you trust me?" Being economically empowered has nothing to do with love or trust. A rejoinder is, "If I have assets in my name, why is that a problem to you?"

3. Financial advisers suggest that enough cash be available to finance six months of living expenses in the event of injury, unemployment or other emergencies.

4. Each party in the relationship should have complete knowledge of the family's assets and financial transactions. Sign tax returns and keep your own copy. Know what investments are made and participate in making them.

5. If there is the possibility of a divorce, find a competent attorney skilled in family law. Go to the library and read up on divorce laws in your state. Talk to others who have been through divorce (there are divorce groups in virtually every town and city).

Although these five points are simple and logical, you may have to struggle to attain each one. Nevertheless, without financial power, the relationship is likely to be skewed and your personal freedom may be compromised.

The next (final) chapter focuses on how to change those aspects of your life that are troubling to you by examining your resistance and world view, and then applying what you have learned in positive ways.

A GUIDE FOR CHANGE

HOW TO APPLY WHAT YOU'VE LEARNED

Now that you know:

1. The ways in which women and men are **different**;

2. How these differences contribute to **misunderstandings**; and

3. **Why** couples don't get along; gender based problems in your relationships can now be dealt with.

Good relationships are not only possible but well within your power. Your new knowledge of *gender differences* increases your personal power and mastery of your relationships by allowing you to:

1. Sort out realistic expectations from those that cannot be realized.

2. Eliminate *interpersonal fog*: (Fog: A mist that envelopes the relationship and eventually becomes impenetrable. You can't talk through it, shout through it, see through it, or hear through it. You can, however, feel the unhappiness and confusion inside the fog.)

With knowledge you can direct your energy to behavior that advances your interests. Specifically, now armed with understanding about the differences between the sexes and a desire to alter your relationship, how do you become the architect of self-change?

KNOW, EVALUATE AND PRIORITIZE YOUR GOALS

What do you want? Is what you want realistic and can you get it from *your* partner?

1. **If you have a vague longing you cannot clearly articulate to yourself, you have little prospect of having your needs met.** "I'm just not happy, there's something missing," is too vague to get the job done. "You just don't turn me on," informs the other person you're dissatisfied but it isn't specific and doesn't allow the other person to respond. Where does this vagueness originate?

There are many adults who have never given up the implicit demand to be understood—just as their care takers understood them when they were babies. When a baby wants something from a parent, the baby doesn't have to be skilled in communication. It's the parents' task to pinpoint the child's needs.

As adults, some people retain child-like attitudes; they *want* and *need* but they do not take responsibility for clearly communicating their "secret" desires. Since *magically* having their mind read worked when they were babies, these adults want to be loved and cared for in the same fashion.

Their attitude is: "I want what I want and I want it now!" A person caught in this time warp is likely to be angry or hurt if asked to clearly specify their desires: "If I have to ask you, it's ruined. You should know without my telling you!" they seem to say.

If your needs aren't met, self-exploration is your first task. Then you will be able to deliver a clear, non-threatening specification of your desires to the person you rely upon for satisfaction. For example, suppose you are unhappy because there's an inner conflict between being a career woman and full time mother. The job interferes with your desire to spend time at home, to nurture your children, and to be the kind of mother you want to be.

Something will have to be given up—career or mothering—or you will be in perpetual conflict. Blaming your husband, who has fathered the children but isn't skilled in parenting them the same way you are, will create turmoil within you and within the marriage.

The dilemma is that you need to add a second income to the family or your standard of living will decline. A further complication is that if you devote all of your time to mothering and do not develop your talents you will miss out on an important source of satisfaction.

"But," you might protest, "if my husband would sacrifice some of his career interests to provide more active parenting, it would make my life easier."

Is he willing to make changes? Are you? Hard choices have to be made and they are sure to be choices with consequences. **This is why you should be clear about your values and be able to prioritize them in importance.**

Remember: the more your happiness and well-being rest upon changes that others must make, the less likely you are to get what you want.

One of our clients came in for counseling because she was divorcing her husband. She wanted to go to college but he wouldn't help with household tasks. When she assessed this situation and decided that college was more important than her high housekeeping standards, she accommodated to whatever help he was willing to provide. It was better, she decided, than being a single parent and doing everything herself.

2. Evaluate the **likelihood of getting what you want in your situation.** If your husband wants to expand his role as parent and he's receptive to reducing his workload for the good of the family, fine. If he isn't, you have to include in your calculations who he is and how likely he is to change—regardless of how unfair it seems.

For example, if you demand empathy and understanding from a man, you create your own problem. "Oh," you say, "but men *should* be more sensitive to women." Yes, they should. If they do not—besides condemning them for their lack of empathy—what can you do about it? We suggest that you give serious consideration to your values, your wishes, your standards and your needs. Avoid *gender conceit*: the hidden, unquestioned assumption that what you feel so strongly about is therefore right and correct for others.

Face it: Men are not trained to be thoughtful and sensitive about anyone—women included. They are taught to deny their feelings. What leads you to expect they will then take your feelings into account?

To improve your emotional ties with a man requires thought and planning. If you need understanding and empathy, bring it to the attention of the resistant person by letting them know this is serious. It's not *just another request* or something on your *wish list.*

Initially, start with a low-keyed but intense talk about this matter. Never raise this issue when there are distractions. A specific time and place should be reserved for this discussion, free of interruptions. Begin with a statement indicating that you have a matter of utmost importance to discuss concerning the future of your relationship.

If you are not able to explain your needs so he understands them, suggest an encounter group, reading material or therapy as a way for both of you to get your messages heard. If he resists, redouble your efforts to GET HIS

ATTENTION. Do not carry on business as usual!
Be prepared to experience and/or create
consequences for his resistance.

This is not the same as nagging, which is a
counter productive strategy. For example, if
you are ignored, announce that you are not
prepared to meet any more of his needs if he
isn't prepared to take yours seriously. If there
are social engagements you are expected to
attend as a happy couple, put them on hold
until the matter you need to have settled is
addressed.

Don't use divorce threats as a ploy. Women
sometimes threaten divorce or let it be known
they have consulted an attorney to gain a man's
attention. This should be a last resort; you
should be prepared to carry it through before
you announce it. More than a few women have
been sorry for using a divorce threat as a ploy
because the man took the threat as a challenge
or an opportunity to end the relationship. His
pride might have been injured or he might
have been wanting out of the relationship all
along.

If you do nothing, or continue the behavior
that hasn't yielded results in the past, you may
have an experience similar to one of our
friends. She told us that for years she sought
companionship and sex from her husband. One
day she approached him while he was lying on
the couch watching TV.

He saw her coming and put his forearm
over his eyes. She stood there for several
minutes debating on a course of action.
Suddenly she had powerful and strange
sensation, "a bodily experience" that all of her

love and interest in him was draining out of her. She left the room without speaking to him and filed for divorce that week.

3. Are your "oughts" and "shoulds" universally true? "You *ought* to remember my birthday if you love me," or "A husband *should* provide a wife with security." However appropriate these standards may seem to you, the question is: How *realistic* are these expectations?

Being taken care of was built into Maureen's life expectations:

> Maureen's sixteen year marriage to Ed, a sometime businessman (2 failures), a real estate agent (13 months), an insurance salesman (18 months), had highs and lows but the lows began to predominate. Ed had thirteen jobs during their marriage, some lasting less than two weeks. He was continually trying to find the "right place" for himself in the world. Meanwhile, Maureen steadily progressed in her occupation. She now consults with three major companies in her area and is in demand in other regions of the country.
>
> Maureen wants to slow down and spend more time at home with the kids. If Ed isn't there to help with the household and add money, how can she? Maureen's complaints are that Ed doesn't hold a job long and isn't available to help with the children on a regular basis.
>
> She doesn't want to continue to turn her three children over to baby-sitters and proxy mothers. It "fries" her when Ed is between jobs, acts depressed, and then develops a passion for his next enterprise only to have it turn sour. Maureen is tired of having her hopes raised then dashed.
>
> Maureen came to counseling because the "D" word—divorce—was now popping into her mind. With careful

evaluation, Maureen discovered she was not only worried about security, she had also absorbed our culture's dictate that requires men to take care of the economic needs of the family. She held this view despite her strong commitment to women's rights and the ideal that women should take care of themselves.

Her father prided himself on how well he took care of the family. Her mother admired him because he properly fulfilled the man's role. Once Maureen recognized her own inconsistencies—she wanted to be a career person but she also wanted to be taken care of—she could resolve the conflict.

The solution? Actually, Maureen's income was sufficient to provide for the family. She had built up long term security by investing wisely in pension plans, IRAs, and annuities. Ed, except for his difficulty sticking to one job, was otherwise a loving husband and father. She realized she was making gender dictated demands. Once she respected who Ed was, the anger and hurt left. She loved him for who he was, not who she wanted him to be.

Ed continued to move from one job to another and Maureen decided to accept this as his pattern. Their relationship and her state of mind improved significantly. Ed felt less a failure in life because he and Maureen now agreed on the kind of person he was.

In response to the changes in his wife's behavior and attitudes, Ed limited his choices to jobs that allowed him to coordinate parenting with Maureen. The life of the entire family improved.

PERCEPTIONS ARE EVERYTHING

Our perceptions shift and change as people in our lives move in different directions and the environment is altered. Sometimes changes occur from profound insights. At other times external events force their way into our lives and change us forever. Most often change comes from an accumulation of experience.

Our world view, although real for us, *is simply our own interpretation of life.* Other people have different perceptions as valid as ours. Neither of you is *right* nor *wrong*. The other person in your life does not have to think, feel, or behave as you do. It is counter productive to force-feed others with your views.

How we view another person's characteristics and behavior (as well as our own), can be a source of pleasure or pain. Personality characteristics or biological differences can be viewed as interesting, aggravating, admirable, disgusting, funny, intolerable, stupid or in a variety of other ways.

This truth—that perceptions vary and are valid for each perceiver—is one of the most difficult ideas to grasp because we live in a world of science and objectivity, black and white, right and wrong, moral and immoral.

"What, I'm supposed to think that things are all relative? But, I can't live my life without some certainty!" If you can accept the fact that **your world isn't the only world**, and that while you share perceptions with others, it is also normal to have differing view, you're actually in a stronger position to determine your fate.

For example, Kramer and Dunaway (1990) argue that one problem men have in understanding women is that women have at least four, not one man, in mind:

1. The hero-warrior-provider
2. The playmate
3. The friend
4. The lover.

If women do not understand the relativity and complexity—even the contradictions—in their own orientation, then how can they get what they want?

A particular man may be good at the provider role but not as a friend. Should this sink the relationship? True, he may not suit a woman who values the "friend-man" more than the "provider man." Then, she will have to make a difficult choice: accommodate, struggle on indefinitely to change him, divorce.

The critical role of *perceptions* came up in a discussion between the authors after we had seen a TV drama in which a woman felt she was raped. The man did not believe he'd raped her. True, he had taken her to his office and commanded her to remove her clothing. She disrobed. He then put on a condom and had sex with her—against her will, as she saw it. Romantically, as he saw it.

He used no weapons or threats but she was fully convinced by his demeanor that if she resisted, her life was in danger. Was this man the rapist she saw him as or the exciting manly lover he thought himself to be?

Can a woman experience rape while the man thinks he's acting in a way to turn them both on? The answer, however unpleasant, is "yes." As we have shown previously, women say "no" in ways men do not comprehend. This might have been the case in the William Kennedy Smith–Pat Bowman case in West Palm Beach (December 1991). The jury decided that there was no rape. We doubt if Ms. Bowman is convinced of that.

Dr. Rhodes believes men must be trained to honor a woman's "no," rather than press on with their agenda. Dr. Goldner agrees and emphasizes that women would benefit from being trained to deliver a much clearer and assertive "NO!" Some women say no and mean yes, some say no and mean no but do not behave in a clear "no" fashion. TV and movies frequently portray women as being ambivalent about their intentions in sexual situations. The mass media thereby add to the problem.

Not only in the sexual area but throughout our lives we are taught that "no" doesn't mean NO. All of us are taught not to take "no" for an answer when pursuing something of value. "Never give up," we're told. And all of us have been told "no" and then gotten our way.

The same confusion is involved in "yes" and other communications. "Oh, you're just saying that" is one expression we use to dismiss the overt message we choose not to accept.

Perspective and interpretations are critical: The sex and gender of the person sending the message or receiving it alters its meaning.

BEGIN NOW, ON YOUR OWN

The gender problems you experience personally and in relationships can best be dealt with by attending to the problem as soon and as effectively as possible, even if it means that you must make the first move."

If you are in a relationship and the other person doesn't want to cooperate or change, why should you? "What? I should make changes while s/he stays the same? Why should I sacrifice if s/he won't?"

Look at it this way: If you change, the system changes; if you change for the better and the other person doesn't, at least you've made progress and the system has been altered. Will it change in the ways you want it to? Not always, but it will change.

We all have complaints about others and want them to be make concessions. But, how practical is this goal? Not very practical if your happiness requires that someone else change before you're satisfied. If it is your desire to improve your own communication skills, you can readily do so if you put out the necessary effort for a sufficient length of time in an efficient manner.

In contrast, imagine that your goal is to motivate someone else to change in ways you desire but they don't. Your task is then substantially complicated and much more likely to fail.

If you view *personal change* as desirable, you have a better chance of getting what you want. But, this means giving up assignment of blame. The more responsible you are for the difficulty in your life, the greater the likelihood you can solve the problem. This is so because it's easier to change yourself than to change others or the world around you.

This self-responsibility theme is extremely difficult to put into practice because it is so natural to blame others for our difficulties. Yet, if you blame others and are convinced they should change to please you, you have created your own dungeon and given the keys to the other person. There's a better way.

Decide RIGHT NOW to be the architect of your life by changing outdated patterns and habitual expectations.

At best, a relationship is an **interdependent system** which can be modified and fine-tuned with both parties in cooperation. What are your alternatives if your spouse isn't making a sufficient effort to improve the relationship? Is all lost? No.

A system is composed of interdependent parts that respond to inner and outer stimuli. If it is functioning well, it adjusts and changes enough to preserve itself. Otherwise, it disappears. This is true of machines, economies, businesses, biological organisms and relationships.

Of what use is this information about systems to someone struggling with an uncooperative mate? **Every part in the system**

(you are a "system part") inevitably influences the rest of the system and its components because any change in one part or function of the system influences all other aspects of the system.

You are already well acquainted with the *negative* effects of system influence. If someone you love or work with is depressed, the emotional contagion affects you, too. Even one dour person can ruin the good time of the group.

If you get a job and have your own income, you immediately increase your power because you have changed the equations in the system. If he reacts by divorcing you, then the system has failed but you still have your gains. You have enhanced yourself, staked out a position in life. You have developed power over yourself and the ability to resist improper power that others exercise over you. You no longer have to quake when you hear the words, "as long as you're living under my roof...."

If your mate responds by adapting to the change in the power arrangement, both of you benefit from the adjustment and the system continues to function.

S/HE MAKES ME MAD!

Another common problem in relationships is that one can be provoked and angered by someone who knows your "weak spots: and "where the skeletons are buried." As one of our clients put it, "I can't win an argument with Matthew. He's just too good at it. Any discussion turns into a debate, then an argument and I end up feeling worse about the argument than my original complaint. *He makes me so mad!*"

Consider this perfect solution to Matthew's provocations: *decide* to not get mad. "But," you might protest, "you are missing the point; he *makes* me mad." Our point is: he does not make you mad, you *choose* to be mad rather than to react in some other way such as having a laughing fit or ignoring him. You don't have to feel threatened, frustrated or angry. If you choose another reaction you automatically and powerfully change the system by not responding to his invitation to fight. How can this be accomplished?

When your mate signals he's inviting you to respond to his provocation, signal to him that you decline. For example, tell him you'll respond when he's ready to *discuss* the issues but you will not participate if he raises his voice, insults you, changes the subject or tries to argue you out of your position.

Tell him that you are willing to engage in a discussion that includes each of you listening to each other's views and opinions. In exchange, he must listen to yours. If he agrees, continue the discussion as long as it is limited to an exchange of opinions without name-calling and other objectionable features.

If there is a deviation from what is acceptable to you—under the terms you previously specified—end your participation. Resume it on condition that game rules are observed. (One helpful rule: You agree to disagree.)

If you follow this line of thought and action, the old system of argumentation ends because you refuse to participate. Then he can no longer "make you mad." You will control your own behavior and he will have to change his or he'll have to find someone else to argue with.

In summary, there are three important steps to take: 1. The first is to develop a different perspective and new information; 2. The second is to apply your new perspective to particular areas of your life; 3. The third is to take action and that inevitably means taking risks.

RESISTANCE TO CHANGE AND FEAR OF NECESSARY RISKS

What makes change so difficult? When we learn something at an early age, everything else builds on that knowledge and way of perceiving. Males and females live in slightly different worlds and therefore, develop different perspectives. No woman knows what it's like to be a man and no man knows what it is like to be a woman. At best they can be empathic with and respect one another.

In infancy we begin to develop a *world view*, a mental road map that channels our thoughts, forms our perceptions, and determines our behaviors. This *world view* directs our construction of reality that in turn becomes a dominant force in our lives.

Although women and men share a common world—this makes social life possible—each has a *sub-world view* specific to his/her own gender. The two sexes see and experience life differently and each has difficulty in understanding the other's experiences. The result is a gap in understanding that is difficult to bridge. Women and men have a strong tendency to think, feel and behave as if their ways, those of their gender, are inherently superior.

THE POWER OF HABIT

Once a world view is established, it is difficult to change because it takes on the attributes of habit. Habit—a pattern in thought, feeling or behavior—is necessary for a stable personality and resists change even when alteration is desired by the conscious mind. Why is habit so resistant to modification?

To become established the habit must provide some reward, even if it is relatively small—like the release of tension with a facial tic. Any habit is woven into the totality of the system which not only tolerates but supports it. "It may be a bad habit, but it's *my* bad habit. If I change it, what then? I'll play it safe and stay as I am.

To end a habit or change a pattern also produces risk and undesirable by products. For example, tobacco smokers often gain weight after giving up nicotine. The weight disturbs

the person's body image. This motivates the
person to resume smoking.

When a change occurs, unpredictable and
undesirable things can happen. The fear of the
unknown is enough to prevent most change.
However, as scary as risk taking may be, by not
taking *calculated* risks you suffer the
consequences of maintaining a dysfunctional
pattern.

If you aren't ready to change undesirable
aspects of yourself (and therefore, the
dysfunctional parts of the system in which you
operate), your life is unlikely to improve. True,
you may decide after careful evaluation that the
present dysfunctional situation is better than
taking the risks involved in change. This may
be the best decision for you. If this is the case,
stop complaining about the other person's
failure to change. Take responsibility for your
own decision and accept the consequences
while moderating them as much as possible.

The *pace of change* is another important
consideration. Every day we are involved in the
never ending process of evolving, accepting,
rejecting, disqualifying, or redefining
ourselves. Nevertheless, efforts to change too
much too soon are doomed to failure. This is as
true of your social or psychological patterns as
it is of your food habits,

Recognize that an individual has limited
capacity to focus and concentrate. Choose the
issues which are essential to your well-being to
work on first. Then allow enough time to make
the change. What if all of *your* efforts are to no
avail? Should you give up?

GET HELP IF YOU NEED IT

Reasons to avoid counseling:

1. We are taught from an early age to keep family secrets. "Don't air your dirty laundry" is a saying meant to instruct family members to conceal difficulties.

2. *Competent* adults can solve all their problems.

3. There used to be a stigma placed upon the "spiritually-possessed-mentally-ill" so we can easily see why people usually avoid, if they can, reliance on therapists.

Our last recommendation: If you try your best and are unable to make satisfactory progress toward your goals, see a therapist. In our psychology practices we find that reading and self–help groups are effective aids to change. They are also excellent adjuncts to individual and couples' therapy.

In short, growth and change come from multiple sources. No one avenue of change is the best or most effective for everyone.

SUMMARY

Gender differences are slight and irrelevant by some standards. What difference should it make if women have slightly better biologically based verbal skills than men? As we have shown, the key to understanding these differences is not in their magnitude but in the importance that people assign to them.

We practice and recommend therapy that is GENDER SENSITIVE AND NO-FAULT. This means that the therapists and the client *respect* differences that are founded on sex (biology) and gender (learning and biology). These differences are not going to be eliminated, so why try? But, the **gender gap** can be bridged. Therapists, as well as clients, need to understand that their own biology and gender influences therapy.

Face the need to change. Implement the ideas offered in this book and those from any other source that is helpful. Gender is a powerful force in our lives. It can separate us or bring us closer together. Let's use our knowledge of sex and gender to enhance our lives.

Take command of Gender Differences to improve and enrich your life!

It's not the end, it's the beginning.

BIBLIOGRAPHY

Abbey, Antonia. 1982. "Sex differences in attributions to friendly behavior: Do males misperceive female's friendliness?" Journal of Personality and Social Psychology, 42, pp. 830-838.

Adler, Tina. 1991, Jan. "Seeing double? Controversial twins study is widely reported, debated."*The APA Monitor*, Vol. 22, No. 1, pp. 1-8.

Arliss, Laurie. 1991. *Gender Communication.* Englewood Cliffs, New Jersey: Prentice Hall.

Barr, Roseanne. 1989. *Roseanne: My Life as a Woman.* New York: Harper & Row.

Barry, Dave. 1989, August 20. "Clearing up the mystery of guy thinking." *Detroit Free Press Magazine,* p. 6.

Baruch, Grace, Barnett, Rosalind, and Rivers, Caryl. 1983. *Lifeprints.* New York: New American Library.

Benderly, Beryl Lieff. 1987. *The Myth of Two Minds.* New York: Doubleday.

Bernard, Jessie. 1972. *The Future of Marriage.* New York: Bantam.

Bernstein, Anne E., & Warner Gloria Marmer. 1984. *Women Treating Women.* New York: International Universities Press.

Bettelheim, Bruno. 1965. "The problem of generations," in E. Erikson (ed.), *The Challenge of Youth.* New York: Doubleday.

Blanchard, Paula. 1990, May 8. "Derivative power still achieves great things." *The Detroit Free Press,* p. 5B.

Blau, Melinda. 1990, December. "Can we talk?" *American Health,* pp. 17-45.

Blood, Robert O. and Donald M. Wolfe. 1960. *Husbands & Wives: The Dynamics of Married Living.* New York: Free Press.

Blurton-Jones, N. G., and M. J. Konner. 1973. "Sex differences in behavior of london and bushman children," pp. 689-750 in Richard P. Michael and John H. Crook, (eds.), *Comparative Ecology and Behavior of Primates*. London: Academic Press.

Buechner, Frederick. 1991. *Telling Secrets*. New York: Harper Collings.

Bugenthal, James F. T. 1987. *The Art Of The Psychotherapist*. New York: W. W. Norton.

Campbell, Ann. 1989. *The Opposite Sex*. Topsfield, Mass: Salem House Printers.

Camus, Albert. 1969. *The Rebel*. New York: Alfred A. Knopf.

Cancian, Francesca M. 1990. *The Feminization of Love*, pp. 171-185 in Christopher Carlson, (ed.) ,*Perspective on the Family*. Wadsworth Publishing Co.: Belmont, California.

Centers for Disease Control Survey. (1989, December 5). *The Detroit Free Press*, p. 14.

Chodorow, Nancy. 1971. "Being and doing: A cross-cultural examination of the socialization of males and females," in Vivian Gornick and Barbara K. Moran (eds.) *Woman in Sexist Society*. New York: Basic Books.

Corliss, Richard. 1989, July 31. When Humor Meets Heartbreak. *Time*, p. 65. (Quote by Rob Reiner, *When Harry Met Sally*).

DeBeauvoir, Simone. 1952. *The Second Sex*. New York: Vintage Books.

Doyle, James A. 1985. *Sex & Gender*. Dubuque, Iowa: Wm. C. Brown Publishers.

Eichenbaum, Luise, and Susie Orbach. 1983. *What Do Women Want*. New York: Berkley Books.

Erikson, Erik H. 1950. *Childhood and Society*. New York: W. W. Norton.

Facts of Life: Love or Lust? 1989, January/February. *Psychology Today*, p. 6.

Farrell, Warren. 1986.*Why Men Are The Way They Are*. New York: McGraw-Hill.

Fausto-Sterling, Anne. 1985. *Myths of Gender*. New York: Basic Books, Inc.

Frankenhauser, Marianne. 1982. "Challenge=control interaction as reflection in sexes." *Scandinavian Journal of Psychology*. Supplement 1, pp. 158-64.

_____. 1978. "Psychoneuroendocrine sex differences in adaptation to the psychosocial environment," in *Clinical Psychoneuroendrinology in Reproduction (Proceedings of the Serono Symposia*, vol. 22). New York: Academic Press.

French, Marilyn. 1985. *Beyond Power*. New York: Summit Books.

_____, 1925. "Some psychical consequences of the anatomical distinction between the sexes," in Vol. XIX.

Gilligan, Carol. 1982. *In a Different Voice*. Cambridge, MA: Harvard University Press.

_____, and Nona P. Lyons and Trudy J. Hanmer. 1990. *Making Connections*. Cambridge, Mass: Harvard University Press .

Halcomb Ruth. 1979. *Women Making It*. New York: Ballantine Book.

Heiman, Julia R. 1980. "Selecting for the sociobiologically fit," in *Behavioral and Brain Sciences*, 3.

Jordan, Judith V. 1987. "Clarity in connection: Empathic knowing, desire and sexuality." *Work in Progress*, 29. Wellesley, Mass: Stone Center Working Papers Series.

Kaplan, Alexandra G. 1984. "The 'self-in-relation': Implications for depression in women." *Work in Progress*, 14. Wellesley, Mass: Stone Center Working Papers Series.

Kinsey, Alfred. 1953. *Sexual Behavior in the Human Female*. Philadelphia: W. B. Saunders.

Kohlberg, Lawrence. 1973. "Continuities and discontinuities in childhood and adult moral development revisited," in *Collected Papers on Moral Development and Moral Education*. Moral

Education Research Foundation. Cambridge, Mass: Harvard University Press.

_____. 1976. "Moral stages and moralization: The cognitive-developmental approach," in T. Lickona, ed., *Moral Development and Behavior: Theory, Research and Social Issues.* New York: Holt, Rinehart and Winston.

Kohn, Alfie. 1988, January 31. "In conversation women do the work and men butt in." *The Detroit Free Press*, p. 1-K.

Kramer, Jonathan and Dunaway, Diane. 1990. *Why Men Don't Get Enough Sex and Women Don't Get Enough Love.* New York: Pocket Star Books.

Lamanna, Mary Ann, and Agnes Riedmann. 1981. *Marriages and Families.*. Belmont, California: Wadsworth Publishing.

Lever, Janet. 1976. "Sex differences in the games children play." *Social Problems*, 23, pp. 478-487.

Levinson, Daniel J. 1978. *The Seasons of a Man's Life.* New York: Alfred A. Knopf.

Levy, J. and M. Reid. 1976. "Variations in writing posture and cerebral organization." *Science* 194. pp. 337-39.

_____. 1981. "Yes, Virginia, there is a difference: Sex differences in human brain asymmetry and in psychology." *The L.S. Leaky Foundation News*, 20 (Fall).

Maccoby, Eleanor, and C. Jacklin. 1974. *The Psychology of Sex Differences.* Stanford, California: Stanford University Press.

McGuinness, Diane. "Sex differences in the organization of perception and cognition," in Lloyd and Archer, pp. 123-56.

McLoughlin, Merrill, with Shryer, Tracy L., Goode, Erica E., & McAuliffe, Kathleen. 1988, August 8. "Men vs. Women." *U.S. News & World Report*, pp. 50-56.

Masters, William H., Virginia E. Johnson, and Robert C. Kolodny. 1982. *Human Sexuality.* Boston: Little, Brown.

Mead, George Herbert. 1967. *Mind, Self, and Society.* Chicago: University of Chicago Press.

Miller, Jean Baker. 1976. *Toward a New Psychology of Women.* Boston: Beacon Press.

_____. 1984. "The development of Women's sense of self." *Work in Progress,* 12. Wellesley, Mass.: Stone Center Working Papers Series.

_____. 1986. "What do we mean by relationships?" *Work in Progress,* 22. Wellesley, Mass.: Stone Center Working Papers Series.

_____. 1988. "Connections, disconnections and violations." *Work In Progress,* 3. Wellesley, Mass.: Stone Center Working Papers Series.

Morris, Jan. 1974. *Conundrum.* New York: Harcourt Brace Jovanovich.

National Crime Survey. 1991, January. *Justice Department.*

Norwood, Robin. 1985. *Women Who Love Too Much.* New York: Simon & Schuster.

Piaget, Jean. 1965. *The Moral Judgment of the Child.* New York: The Free Press.

Richardson, Joan. 1990, June 24. "A most disciplined divorce." (Paula Blanchard). *Detroit Free Press Magazine.*

Rubin, Lillian B. 1979.*Women of a Certain Age.* New York: Harper & Row.

Rutter, M., and H. Giller. 1984. *Juvenile Delinquency: Trends and Perspectives.* New York: Guilford Press.

Sarnoff, Irving, and Suzanne Sarnoff. 1989, October. "The dialectic of marriage." *Psychology Today,* pp. 54-57.

Sartre, Jean-Paul. 1964. *The Words.* New York: Fawcett.

Scanzoni, Letha, and John H. Scanzoni. 1976. *Men, Women & Change: A Sociology of Marriage and Family.* New York: McGraw-Hill.

Schlafly, Phyllis. 1988. The power of the positive woman. In Kurt Finsterbusch and George McKenna (ed.), *Taking Sides.* (5th ed.), pp. 76-82. Guilford, Ct: Dushkin Publishing.

Segell, Michael. 1989, January/February. "The American man in transition." *American Health,* pp. 59-61.

Strachey, James. 1934. *Complete Psychological Works of Sigmund Freud,* trans. and ed. London: The Hogarth Press.

Stiver, Irene. 1984. "The meanings of 'dependency,' in female-male relationships." *Work in Progress.* Wellesley, Mass.: Stone Center Working Papers Series.

Surrey, Janet L. 1984. "Eating patterns as a reflection of women's development." *Work in Progress,* 83-86. Wellesley, Mass: Stone Center Working Papers Series.

_____. 1985. "Self-in-relation: A theory of women's development." *Work in Progress,* 13. Wellesley, Mass: Stone Center Working Papers Series.

Symons, Donald. 1979. *The Evolution of Human Sexuality* . New York: Oxford University Press.

Tanenbaum, Joe. 1989. *Male & Female Realities.* Sugarland, Texas: Candle Publishing Co.

Tannen, Deborah. 1990. *You Just Don't Understand.* New York: William Morrow.

Travis, Carol, and Wade, Carole. 1984. *The Longest War.* San Diego: Harcourt Brace Jovanovich.

U.S. Bureau of Justice Statistics, Washington, DC: *U.S. Uniform Crime Reports,* 1991. U.S. Government Printing Office, pp. 69-90.

Virginia Slims American Women's Opinion Poll, 1974, 1985.

West, Candance, and Don Zimmerman. 1977. "Women's place in everyday talk: Reflections on parent-child interaction." *Social Problems.* 24, pp. 521-29.

Williams, J. E. 1982. "An overview of findings from adult sex stereotype studies in 25 countries," in *Diversity and Unity in Cross-Cultural Psychology*. Edited by R. Rath, H. S. Asthana, D. Sinha, and J. B. Sinha. Lisse, The Netherlands: Swets and Zeitlinger. et al.

Witelson, Sandra F. 1976. "Sex and the single hemisphere: Specialization of the right hemisphere for spatial processing." *Science*, 193, pp. 425-427.

Young-Bruehl, Elisabeth. 1990. *Freud on Women*. New York: W. W. Norton & Co.

Young-Eisendrath, Polly, and Wiedemann, Florence. 1984. *Female Authority*. New York: The Gilford Press.

FEEDBACK CORNER

Dr. Goldner and Dr. Rhodes would like to hear from you: what is your reaction to the material in this book? What experiences have you had that confirm, contradict or can enlarge our understandings?

If you are agreeable to the use of your responses in our next book, please so specify. (We will use your story in ways that will guarantee your anonymity.)

Whenever possible, we will reply to your questions and comments.

Thanks for reading *WHY WOMEN AND MEN DON'T GET ALONG*. We hope you enjoyed our book as much as we enjoyed writing it.

Send your comments to us C/O Somerset Publishing, P.O. Box 4386, Troy, MI 48099

ORDER EXTRA COPIES OF

WHY WOMEN AND MEN DON'T GET ALONG

BY
CAROL L. RHODES, PH.D.
AND
NORMAN S. GOLDNER, PH.D.

SOMERSET PUBLISHING COMPANY
P.O. BOX 4386
TROY, MI 48099

Please send a copy of **Why Women and Men Don't Get Along**. I enclose $10.95 + $3.05 to cover shipping, packaging, and handling. a total of $14.00, CHECK OR MONEY ORDER, payable to Somerset Publishing, P.O.B. 4386, Troy, MI 48099

Ship to NAME:_____

ADDRESS_____

CITY_____STATE_____ZIP_____